ALSO BY JEFFRY C. BEERS

The Lost Season

The New Season: Journey Toward Enlightenment

Peace: The Art of Mindfulness to Eliminate Stress

Presence: The Art of Living in the Now

Creation: The Art of Manifesting Desires

Zen: The Art of Conscious Living

For More Writings Please Visit:

www.zen-professor.com

PEACE

The Art of Mindfulness to Eliminate Stress

JEFFRY C. BEERS

TRAVELING AT LIFE'S SPEED
Book 1

Beers, Jeffry C.
Peace: The Art of Mindfulness to Eliminate Stress

Printed in the United States of America
First Printing, 2016

ISBN-10: 978-1512344158

The Power Center Publishing, LLC
4820 NE Hazel Dell Ave, #534
Vancouver, WA 98663

TRAVELING AT LIFE'S SPEED
Series Introduction

"If you want to know your past life, look into your present condition; if you want to know your future life, look at your present actions."

- Padmasambhava

Dearest Reader,

I have written this book series in order to share what I have learned over the past ten years. Before becoming an author, I was a public school teacher for 25 years, the first 20 of which were spent coaching in multiple sports. During that time I basically worked 60 to 70 hours per week. In 2007, after a very frustrating season, I began to ponder whether I wanted to continue coaching.

One day, I was sitting by a pond watching the world go by. I noticed a dragonfly clinging desperately to the stem of a leaf in an attempt to keep from being blown away by the wind. I could sense how it felt. Perhaps we all could. It let go and made a small circle in the air before returning home to cling desperately once again. That dragonfly seemed to be talking to me, instructing me that I had been limiting my experience. In that moment I decided I was going to start making bigger circles in my life. I wanted to notice more of what was going on around me and what I had missed up to that point.

For 20 years I was a full-time teacher and coach. I had coached basketball, tennis, football, and track during that portion of my career, so finding time to sit by a pond and watch the world go by was something new to me. I began to wonder, how many of us have limited our circle of life by getting set in our ways and failing to venture out. I knew that in my personal experience so much time was spent teaching and coaching that little was left to explore new avenues. I decided I wanted to change that. So, I elected to hang up my coaching whistle for a while and explore other facets of life.

After spending several months going on walks, riding my bike, and journaling thoughts, I decided I wanted to go back to grad school and work on a PhD in psychology. In the spring of the first year in grad school I took a class in Contemplative Education and discovered mindfulness. Interestingly, I had already been practicing mindfulness for a little over a year without realizing it, by meditating, reading about living in the present moment, and practicing what I learned. In this book series, *Traveling at Life's Speed,* I hope to use my experience in education, coaching, and life in general, to teach what I discovered about going with the Universal flow and traveling, not at the speed of humanity, but rather, at the speed of life itself.

During the year between coaching and graduate school, I was amazed to realize how much time was available to me after teaching a full day of school. Since I no longer had coaching responsibilities, I was able to be home shortly after 4pm, leaving a great deal of time to do what I wanted. But what, exactly, did I want to do? At the time I wasn't really sure, so I just began reading books and reflecting on what I read. Because I was interested in psychology, and because I was searching to find myself, I read a lot of inspirational books relating to psychology and inner growth.

Two things really stood out to me. The first was simple yet quite profound. I read several books written by Wayne Dyer and it seemed every book I read the author stated the importance of meditating daily. I kept hearing over and over, meditate daily, meditate daily. So, I decided I would meditate daily. At first I found it to be quite difficult to sit still for any given period of time. After all, I had conditioned myself to remain busy always. If I wasn't teaching or coaching I was thinking about teaching and coaching. However, after several weeks of practice I began to get the hang of it, which is to say, I became more comfortable sitting quietly and watching the thoughts go by.

The second aspect of all the reading that really stood out was not quite so simple but even more profound. I started a "book trail," meaning that each time I read a book, I made a note of the publications used by that author that I resonated with most. Next, I went to the library and checked out those books and read them as well. I found myself reading not only modern works on personal growth and development, but also volumes of ancient literature, such as the Bhagavad-Gita and the story of Krishna, dating back as far as 1,500 to 3000 BC. In the story, Krishna (who was portrayed as God in human form) was acting as a spiritual advisor for Arjuna, a prince being faced with the prospect of fighting against friends and family in a war of two great armies. Throughout the story Krishna discussed the psychological and spiritual impact of the choices we make in life.

In addition to reading the philosophy of Krishna, I also read that of the Buddha, Confucius, and Socrates. What I found startled me. Overall, although these three wise souls lived in far different regions with vastly differing cultures, they were pretty much saying the same thing, and I found it to be strikingly similar to what Krishna had said a thousand years or more before they began their teachings. In addition, they all lived around the same time, somewhere around 500 BC. How that information was disseminated around the world during the same era in a time when there was no worldwide travel was beyond me. But there seemed to be something very significant about it.

Moreover, I began to compare what I was reading to the teachings of Jesus Christ, who began his ministry some 500 years later. What struck me was that if we read each of these teachings from the perspective of consciousness, we can see that the meaning beneath the words holds true for all of humanity, not just Christians, or Buddhists, or Muslims, or Hindus, or any other religious sect for that matter. It seems to be the interpretation of these words that leads to division, not the teachings themselves.

It is not the goal here to convince you that all these ideologies are basically the same. There are many others much more qualified than myself who have written volumes on the subject. Instead, I hope to summarize much of the wisdom these great teachers have attempted to impart on us in a way that is easy to read and practical to apply in our daily lives.

In order to tackle what seems like such a monumental task, I intend to talk from a perspective that we are all basically the same. We come from the same place, physically, emotionally, and energetically, and we will return to the same place when our current life story comes to an end. I do not mean to presume I know you, dear reader, any more than you know yourself. I do, however, mean to say that we, as humans, all have the same basic thoughts and feelings, ordered in relation to our vastly differing experiences. Once we begin to look for our similarities above and beyond our differences, our lives will become more peaceful and fulfilling, without the need to fight for our very existence. Because of this viewpoint, I will be speaking mostly from the place of we and us rather than you and me, unless of course I am sharing a personal story or story shared to me by another.

In addition, I do not intend on coming from any religious platform. When referring to the teachings of Krishna, or Buddha, or Christ, I will be describing the stories in terms of what they mean to human consciousness, rather than what they mean in terms of behavior or moral code. Further, because the term "God" comes with so many different connotations, I will be using the word "Universe" instead, unless I am referring to the ideas of others. If the word is capitalized it means *everything* in the Universe, including all physical and energetic properties, whereas, if it is written with a small "u" it is referring to physical plane only. If the reader wants to substitute the word God in place of Universe, it would work just fine. It must be remembered, however, I am coming from the place that we are all from the same unified source energy in body, mind, and consciousness.

In this book series I have described a path to total self-awareness. For me, it all started with reading inspirational literature, contemplative walking, introspective reflecting and journaling. In the first book of the series, *Peace: The Art of Mindfulness to Eliminate Stress,* I wrote about mindfulness and how we can program the mind to change our default progressively from constant mind chatter, to less inner dialog, to mindful chatter, to mostly silent with intentionally directed internal dialog.

These mindful practices help us to discover the silent witness in us all, which is referred to as the "authentic self" and discussed in detail in book two of the series, *Presence: The Art of Living in the Now.* In book three of the series, *Creation: The Art of Manifesting Desires,* I demonstrate that, by coming from the place of present moment awareness, we are able to access our natural creative ability to attract the life we want. *Zen: The Art of Conscious Living,* book four of the series, demonstrates how we can take it a step further and live in continuous peace by changing our baseline awareness from object to space consciousness, allowing us to free the mind, follow our bliss, and live in the reality that we create.

Throughout the series, I have explained how to transcend the psychological self or the ego, which can be fully discovered through mindfulness practice and meditation. I hope that you will be able to keep an open mind to the ideas I have shared. Furthermore, I sincerely desire that by reading the information provided here, you will be inspired to look deeper within yourself and discover the innate wisdom that was provided to us all at birth.

TABLE OF CONTENTS

PREFACE

"The skill of letting go can be learned; once learned you will enjoy living much more spontaneously." — *Deepak Chopra*

As suggested in the quote above, letting go can be learned. A major aspect of digesting emotions is letting go of thoughts leading to suffering. One way to do that is to turn into the emotion rather than away from it. However, it is not easy to learn to face emotions when we have created a habit of turning away from them through distractive measures (referred to as avoidance in the psychological literature). This is what Carl Jung was alluding to when he wrote, "One does not become enlightened by imagining figures of light, but by making the darkness conscious… This procedure, however, is disagreeable and therefore not very popular." In the following chapters I hope to demonstrate that facing emotions is a great way to process or "digest" them, as Jung once referred to it.

So the question is, why is it so difficult to face emotions? To me, the answer is in our relationship to them, which is to say, the thoughts about them. It is the thoughts about the emotions that cause us to turn away. After all, the emotions themselves are nothing more than energy coursing through the body. We have learned, through previous psychological conditioning that some emotions are "good" and others are "bad." Furthermore, the good emotions are to be approached or sought out, and the bad emotions are to be avoided at all costs. What I am suggesting is this ideology is the core of the problem of destructive emotions.

It may be beneficial then, to shape beliefs by letting go of judgments of big and small, good and bad, attractive and ugly, and the like. We can begin to see everything in its entirety by perceiving objects in their relationship to the whole, rather than in contrast to everything else. This is the beginning of freedom from the egoic belief system. However, in order to become free of it, we must first become aware of its existence, which we can do with present moment awareness.

Being present in the now means to be aware of the thoughts and emotions as they arise in the body, without judging them as good or bad. Indeed, thoughts, in and of themselves, are benign. It is from past experience that we give meaning to them by attaching previously felt emotions and storing them in memory. With practice, we can all become much more present in each moment and as a result, live a life of authenticity. The alternative is to come from the place of the psychologically programmed egoic self, simply referred to as the ego.

It has been postulated that humans are the only animal to possess an ego, and therefore, are the only organisms on earth that do not live in the "real" world. What this means is that we are so conditioned by societal beliefs that we become absolutely unaware that the actions and behavior tendencies are not coming from the deeper, inner self, which I like to refer to as the "authentic self." Instead, we are largely extrinsically motivated by society to behave in ways that fits the social and cultural norms of any given community.

Each community typically adopts a general ideology that has been handed down through the ages by their ancestors. Of course, the nuances of each belief system change over time, but by and large the overarching societal structure can remain intact for many generations, at times even for thousands of years. However, times are changing rapidly, and in order to keep up with this metamorphosis, we must learn to adapt to new ideology that more closely fits with the ever-changing environment.

Because many of our beliefs today are based largely on a patriarchic ideology, prominently handed down through the church doctrine of the past, I like to refer to this overarching system of belief as "Father Culture," capitalized to signify its far reaching effects. Each individual then, has his psyche conditioned by Father Culture in a way that *seems* to serve society best. However, as seen by many examples of atrocities committed by populations against one another throughout the ages, this "groupthink" mentality can have major detrimental effects. All one must do to realize this is to recall regimes of the past such as Nazi Germany and the Communist reign of Stalin, along with the more recent genocides in Bosnia and Rwanda.

It must be remembered, however, that the leaders of the countries mentioned above could not perform such atrocities alone; rather, they must have the support of a large number of people in order to carry out these heinous plans. In order to do so, these

5

charismatic personalities were capable of manipulating the minds of those who became willing participants in the regimes' system of destruction. Certainly it was not the authentic selves of the individuals who partook in such madness; rather, it was the egoic selves whose psyches were conditioned to believe that Father Culture knows best. It is for this reason that I refer to the conditioned psyches as their "psychological selves."

The psychological self is built by a lifetime of meaning making experiences that are heavily influenced by the emotions of the body. Once the philosophical system is in place it becomes extremely difficult to become free of it. However, although difficult, it is definitely possible. With a little perseverance and dedication, anyone can learn how to become liberated from the debilitating effects of destructive emotions.

I am not saying that we are currently programmed in a way to partake in atrocities like those referred to above. Nonetheless, we are certainly conditioned in a way that leads us away from the authentic self and toward the societally directed mentality of the psychological self. Because this line of thinking imposes limits on the authentic self, it is imperative we gain an understanding of how to be free of it. In turn, we can live the kind of authentic life we were meant to live. That is the goal of this book.

Before discussing the process of digesting emotions, let's consider what it would be like to see a rope laying on the ground and mistake it for a snake. What would happen to the internal world? The heart may begin to race, the muscles might contract, and we may begin to perspire as the body prepares for flight or fight. The heart may even stop completely as we are overtaken from fear of something that was never there in the first place. The experience of reality, therefore, is based on judgments and beliefs. We believe the rope is a snake, we believe snakes may harm us, and the body reacts according to these beliefs, whether or not they are real.

Once we become aware of the presence of erroneous thinking, we can then begin to process the emotions associated with it. In the example of the rope laying on the ground, upon realizing that the rope is not a snake, we can turn all attention to the feelings in the body that have arisen in relation to the thoughts of snake danger. By keeping attention on the feeling rather than the thoughts that created it, we can feel the emotions fully and allow them to leave the body. That is the central thesis of this book, how to digest emotions so that we can release the energy stirred by them.

What is happening to us in the example cited above is due to the functioning of the sympathetic and parasympathetic nervous systems. The sympathetic nervous system is often referred to as the "hot system," and becomes active during the fight, flight or freeze stage, such as what might happen if we come across a real snake. The hot system becomes active when the individual feels threatened and becomes emotionally charged, creating bodily changes to respond to a stimuli, such as increased heart rate, increased blood flow to the periphery, and a narrowing of focus to the object of attention.

In the fight, flight, or freeze stage, the sympathetic nervous system is preparing the body to act, which means we are preparing to stand *our* ground and fight against a perceived threat, or turn and run away. Or, it is possible that becoming very still and not moving will protect us. It is theorized that this is a method used by prey as a means of hoping to not be seen by a predator. This phenomenon can be seen in the human psyche by observing the intensely shy person who stands in the corner, hoping not to be seen by others. In the case of animals in nature, the freeze method can be used to preserve the physical self. In terms of the human psyche, it is often used to protect the psychological self.

In contrast to the sympathetic nervous system, the parasympathetic nervous system causes the bodily processes to slow down and return to a relaxed state. During the return to homeostasis the attention broadens once again to the entire environment. It is for this reason that centering attention on open space can bring us to a relaxed state very quickly. By centering awareness on space and broadening our perspective, we are activating the parasympathetic nervous system causing the body to relax.

In the paragraphs above, I have outlined briefly what happens to the body in the present moment according to the direction of attention (i.e., object focus engages the sympathetic nervous system, whereas space focus engages the parasympathetic nervous system). However, it doesn't take long before memory becomes engaged and the present moment sensations in the body turn into emotions from past/future thinking. Therefore, memory plays an important role when it comes to processing emotions.

In the book *Measuring the Immeasurable,* Hanson discussed the difference between explicit and implicit memory, with explicit being a simple recollection and factual knowledge, while implicit involves emotions, a sense of the world, and behavioral strategies. The author also discussed life experience in terms of physical and psychological by comparing the saying, "we are what we eat" with the phrase "we are what we remember." He went on to suggest that just as food is incorporated into the physical self, so too is memory incorporated into the psychological self.

During the process mentioned above, the hippocampus of the brain compares current perceptual information with memory and when it discerns a match it sends a signal to the amygdala to warn the entire system (if the match was perceived as a threat). In this way, we don't just go looking for negative experiences, we store these experiences in memory (via the hippocampus-amygdala circuitry) and hold on to it indefinitely. This seems to be where tapping (utilized in energy psychology) comes in, as it seems to release the stored energy by alerting the system that "all is well, the threat has passed, stand down."

Tapping is a method of stress relief in which the individual taps different locations of the body while repeating a phrase of acceptance. It seems to work like acupuncture in that blocked energy in specific locations of the body can be released; bringing the energy system has a whole back into balance. I don't use the technique myself because the process of digesting emotions by centering awareness on them seems to do the trick. However, I know many people who benefit from tapping and it might be worth a try if you are so inclined to learn about it (see Emotional Freedom Technique, or EFT online). In the following chapters, I will explain the process of digesting emotions *before* the energy becomes blocked and *before* other methods such as tapping or acupuncture become necessary.

CHAPTER 1
Digesting Emotions

According to Deepak Chopra the body is perfectly set up to live in the present moment and attain its greatest joy and satisfaction there because it is biologically equipped to handle a broad scope of pressures. Chopra refers to this as the "wisdom of uncertainty." The author goes on to suggest that the same is not the case for the mind because it is more difficult for it to accept uncertainty. The author writes, "It [the mind] fears change, loss, and death. This is the source of resistance, which the body translates into stress. By imposing mental resistance, you create a threat your body has to deal with." Therefore, we must learn to let go of this resistance by turning attention to it without thinking about why it is there.

Outside the present moment the body contracts in the form of emotions. In the present moment the body expands in the form of joy. Thriving is the natural flow of life. When we are in the absolute present moment of now, energy flows undaunted. That is what is meant to be free. What are we free from? We are free from past regrets and future worries. Being free of mental constructs such as these, as well as the stored energy of the emotions associated with them, is what it means to be "enlightened." Enlightened means both the light of awareness is shining brightly, and one is lighter because she is not carrying around past emotional "baggage."

The "God experience" is the feeling of expansion, whereas the "ego experience" is the feeling of contraction. This is where the phrase "edge God out" comes from when considering what is meant by the ego. When we experience the egoic reactions of the body through the stored energy of emotions we feel heavier because the body is contracting. When we experience the authenticity of the deeper self, energy is allowed to flow freely, causing us to feel lighter due to the expansion of energy.

When we "digest" emotions it is much like how the winter snow melts away when the sun shines upon it. If we can be as patient as the sun we can remain at peace while we wait. This is the enlightened state. However, in order to properly digest the emotions we must learn how to let go of the ego.

I am reminded of the old Eggo Waffle commercials in which two people reach for and grab a waffle at the same time, and then one says, "Hey, let go of my Eggo!" Perhaps this would be a good slogan for us all to use by simply changing it slightly to "Let go of my ego!" and turn the phrase inward rather than outward, thereby instructing ourselves to let go of the ego and act from the authentic self, rather than from the perspective of the self-destructing ways of habitual thoughts and actions.

Perhaps a personal story will help to clarify the process of digesting emotions. Six years ago I was having a conversation with a good friend of mine and she asked me about the marriage and subsequent divorce I experienced. Typically, a thought like that would generate a lot of disturbing emotions. However, this time there was no feeling whatsoever. After she noticed the lack of emotional reaction and asked me about it, I shared a theory of mine that I was testing. The theory was that I could become aware of the disturbing emotion as it arises, understand that it is not me and accept it as it is. In turn, the energy associated with the emotion would dissipate rather quickly. When I say dissipate I mean disappear as if it was never there in the first place. This is far different than suppressing it.

When we suppress a thought or emotion we force it to surrender and it does surrender, but it doesn't go away. It merely slips under the radar and can come back at any moment, usually when we least expect it. Many times it is disguised in a different form so we don't even recognize it. For example, let's say a person says something to us that we interpret as an insult and we think something like, "That really hurt! Why did he say that to me?" Pretty soon we are carrying on a detailed conversation in the head, trying to explain what just happened. After a while we grow tired of the contracting feeling caused by the emotion and say something like, "I shouldn't feel that way. Stop feeling that way!" In this way we haven't accepted it but merely suppressed it.

Later, another person comes up and makes an innocent comment and we might jump all over her. She may say something that, in and of itself appears to be quite harmless. However, because we have the energy from the previous encounter stored in the body, we immediately turn attention to any aspect of the comment that may relate to the internal reaction and all of the pent up energy comes pouring out. Sometimes we might even say to ourselves something like, "Wow, where did that come from?"

13

On the other side of the equation we have a far different scenario. If when the original comment was made we become aware of the energy arising in us and separate ourselves from it, causing it to dissipate, then the energy is allowed to leave the body. Because of acceptance, the energy is no longer there to wreak havoc in a later encounter with another poor unsuspecting individual.

The old adage is to "think before you act." However, perhaps it should be to feel before you think, that is to say, we must first turn attention to the internal reaction and after digesting it, only then ask, what might have been the cause of that?

Consider what it means to "swallow your pride." To me, this seems to be a good example of suppressing emotions because it connotes the use of self-regulation in order to control behavior, such as to swallow our pride before going to someone to apologize for a perceived wrongdoing. I suggest there is a technique that helps to release the emotion rather than suppress it.

Instead of "swallowing our pride," we can simply breathe it out. Yes it is merely a change in semantics but words are powerful. Swallowing something connotes taking it in. Obviously, breathing out is the opposite of that. If we tell ourselves we are letting go of the feeling in the breath, we will be more likely to activate the relaxation response discussed earlier through acceptance. Then, we can go to the person to make amends in the absence of any stored emotion that could cloud our judgment.

According to Bruce Lipton, "All of the people we have ever engaged with over our lifetime were also responding using invisible behavioral programs downloaded into their infant subconscious minds." Keeping this in mind, does it not make it easier to observe the emotional reaction in others without taking it personal? Lipton went on to write, "We have all been shackled with emotional chains wrought by dysfunctional behaviors programmed by the stories of the past." Again, this seems to highlight the importance of understanding that the mind and body respond to an event similarly, irrespective of whether it is real or imaginary.

Before going any further in discussing how to process emotions, and the importance of doing it in the present moment, I must first establish that I will be coming from the perspective that, like thoughts, emotions are neither good nor bad, they are simply energy flowing through the body. It is of vital importance to begin labeling them differently. In turn, we can remove any negative connotations that have been attached to the emotions through previous conditioning.

Emotions deemed as negative such as anger, anxiety, and frustration can be seen as emergency emotions. We do, after all, have these emotions for a reason, and they are to be called upon in times of immediate and quite temporary events. The energy arising from anger, for example, can be resourced in time of self-defense or the protection of those who cannot defend themselves. The trouble comes when we attempt to use these emotions when it is not an emergency. In these non-emergency situations, the anger gets released on those not deserving of it or in need of the energy from that particular emotion.

Indeed, how many times have you witnessed or been the recipient of displaced anger from another? Or, perhaps you may remember a time when you yourself have inadvertently misplaced your anger. For example, I remember past times when I seemed to be angered or frustrated at the drop of a hat. In short order I have recognized the pent up energy stemming from being hungry. The moment I have something to eat the emotional arousal ceases to exist, almost as if a switch had been turned off.

One way to remove the negative connotations of the emotion is to notice when it arises and label it "feeling." However, this takes time. It must be remembered that we typically have much practice in labeling emotions. Therefore, it stands to reason that a similar amount of practice will need to go in to removing those labels. Once we have done this, we are free to witness it without judging it as good or bad. In turn, it becomes much easier to stay with the feeling while it occurs, rather than turn away from it and miss the opportunity to process it fully.

After changing the label from any given emotion to feeling, we can begin to see emotion in its true light, as energy. When we remove the negative connotations and recognize the emotion is nothing more than energy flowing through the body it actually feels warm, exciting, comforting, and joyous, even if we previously thought of the feeling as negative and something we did not want. For example, once when I was playing in a band and we were performing in front of people I noticed feelings arise while on the way to the performance. By that time I had been practicing digesting

16

emotions for several years. In turn, what would have been previously labeled as nervousness was felt without the label appearing and, consequently, it didn't feel "bad" at all; rather, I would have to say it felt exciting or invigorating. Naturally that made the event much more enjoyable.

Once we change the mindset to understanding that emotions are nothing more than energy we can let them flow and let them go. It is the thinking about *why* we are feeling it that traps the energy and keeps it from flowing freely. The more we try and evaluate why we are feeling that way, the more energy that gets fed into the current bodily response. For example, when we are feeling angry, the mind conjures up thoughts that were attached to previous events similar to the current one. In turn, energy is added to the present moment occurrence and the emotions become exacerbated.

In their book *The Mind of the Soul*, Gary Zukav and Linda Francis suggest to try an experiment. Whenever we react to anything we are asked to say to ourselves, "I have encountered a frightening part of my personality," then make a note of *what* we reacted to and *how* we reacted. Notice the writers didn't say to write down *why* we reacted. This is what many of us get wrapped up in, the *why* in things.

As soon as we ask ourselves why, we create a nice neat little story in the head. The problem is it's just that, a story. It's not reality. Often times it is far from reality. And often times we make up a worst case scenario and carry this story in our head for days, months, or even years. If, however, we merely notice what we

17

reacted to and how we reacted, without attempting to explain why it happened, we would be free to choose independent of the emotional charge all that thinking is sure to conjure up, assuming of course, that we digest the emotion fully before acting.

I would suggest changing one thing, however, when we are in the process of noticing our reactions. Rather than say "a frightening part…" I would suggest we say, "an interesting part." In turn, we can lessen the self-imposed judgment and increase the likelihood we are not acting from a place of fear. It is important that we keep the inner dialog directed toward where we want to go rather than where we were.

One important aspect to remember about digesting emotions is to be mindful of follow up thoughts; that is to say, thoughts that piggyback on the original thought that triggered the emotion. The reason for this is simple. If we give attention to follow up thoughts it is very likely to increase the emotional disturbance we are feeling. The reason this is so is because each thought after an emotion arousing thought is very likely to have been tagged with a similar emotion from a previous experience. In turn, similar thoughts continue to feed the emotion in the present moment and, rather than experience only present moment sensations, we are forced to come up against past emotions as well, complicating the situation.

It is best to view that emotion for what it is, energy. We can then purposefully feel that energy and refuse to label or judge it as good or bad. In a short period of time, that energy usually flows right through the body and dissipates completely. It is then easier to choose to act in a rational way to address the event which brought on the emotion, or to simply let it go, depending on which decision serves us best.

CHAPTER 2

The Subtleties of Emotions

Before discussing the subtleties of emotions I would like to distinguish between feelings, emotions, and inner sensations. Typically, the word feeling is used interchangeably to cover both inner sensations and emotions. It is helpful to remember that physical sensations (both internal and external) tell us what is happening in real time, whereas, emotions tell us what we are still carrying around from the past. It seems as though the emotions actually lie to us because we could become angry with another and later find out it had nothing to do with that person. However, they do not. It is our erroneous belief that attributes emotions to present moment awareness. The difficulty is in learning to tell the difference.

In order to recognize the difference between inner sensations and emotions, we must recognize the emotional charge when it occurs and give it attention while it is there. Then, after releasing it, we can find its origin by searching the memory banks. Later, when the thought of the current situation returns, it will come in the absence of the emotional charge and we are left with only the sensations of the present circumstances. These sensations are difficult to describe of course, because they are so much subtler. However, with practice, we can learn to discern between the two.

When we follow the sensations it has more to do with the direction we are headed. Conversely, when we are following the guidance of the emotions we are giving more attention to where we *were*. In turn, if we chose to follow the emotions as a guide we would be operating from a place of the psychological self. In short, following sensations allows us to come from a place of curiosity and excitement, the state of the authentic self. However, following the emotions leads us to the ego only.

When we become accustomed to noticing the subtlest levels of feelings (including both sensations and emotions) we can come into contact with what was described more than 2,000 years ago in the Yoga Sutras by Patanjali who wrote: "The totality of creation is experienced as clear or pure to those who have completely unmade their self-destructive internal programs. Being completely free from stress on the inside, they see only Beauty and Truth outside." This is one of the great benefits of learning how to digest the emotions. We simply get to experience more beauty in life because we are better prepared to notice it.

After becoming adept at digesting the emotions we can become more aware of the subtle sensations that underlie thoughts, sometimes referred to as a "hunch" or a "suspicion." I would like to take a moment to explain here that I will be using the word intuition different than hunch or suspicion. It's all a matter of semantics but in order to add clarity into the subtleties of noticing underlying sensations, it helps to distinguish between suspicion and intuition in the same way that we earlier distinguished between emotion and sensation.

The key to understanding lies in the difference between present moment awareness and past/future thinking. Like feelings and emotions, the words feeling and sensation are often used interchangeably, but for the purpose of this exposition I am using sensation only in terms of a bodily response that occurs in the moment upon a sudden realization. In other words, both words come with no connotations of negative or positive, pleasant or unpleasant, strong or mild, etc. However, feeling is an umbrella term that captures them all, including those that occur in the present moment, as well as those that occur over a period of time. In contrast, a sensation occurs in the present moment only.

Similarly, intuition refers to the sudden realization itself. In contrast, when referring to a hunch or suspicion I mean that it is an understanding that occurs over a longer period of time. In other words, an intuition comes with a sensation that occurs in the present moment, whereas, like an emotion, a suspicion occurs over a period of time and is in past/future thinking. First we have an intuition, then, after it gets mixed with thought, it becomes a suspicion. Therefore, a suspicion or hunch is likely to be erroneous because it includes the past/future thinking of egoic belief.

For example, we may have a suspicion that we are not going to pass a class, or not going to get a coveted job, or the car we want. This suspicion comes from past conditioning when the environment failed to meet our expectations. If the emotions experienced from that disappointment have not been fully processed, a residual energy is left behind, and in the future when a similar situation presents itself, this residual energy will begin to rise, creating a suspicion. If that energy goes unnoticed, it stirs a memory of the past event. Next,

22

the memory creates thoughts. The more thoughts that are produced the more energy is stirred, eventually turning it into an emotion. It is in the early phases of the stirring of energy that we begin to become aware of as consciousness expands. In turn, we can direct the attention to the subtle underlying sensation before it can become an emotion.

Sensation comes first, along with intuition. If left unattended, the intuition turns into suspicion, the sensation into emotion, and now we are no longer living in the present moment. Instead, we are living in past/future thinking and are coming from the psychological self. This is what we are trying to head off when we become more sensitive to the underlying feelings that are present, whether they are a present moment sensation, or the residual energy from a previous event.

We could say that becoming more aware of the subtle underlying feelings comes with both "good" and "bad" news. The good news is the recognition that the underlying feeling is present. This indicates that consciousness is indeed expanding. The bad news is the presence of the doubt or fear in the first place. However, if we routinely replace the doubting and fearful thoughts with their opposites, such as what we have and want instead of what we lack and don't want, the thought train will slowly change tracks. Although this is merely at the superficial level of the mind, with time and practice, deeper levels will be reached.

Indeed, it is necessary to search deeper to eliminate the feeling of fear, doubt, anxiety, anger, etc. In order to do that, we must notice the feeling when present, and introduce an uplifting thought *before* the disruptive thought manifests. In turn, consciousness will expand and fear will dissolve. It then becomes much more likely that we will attract that which we want into this life experience.

In reality, there really is no bad news at all. The good news of the expanded consciousness that has already occurred, allowing us to recognize the underlying feeling and stay with it, outweighs any harmful outcome that could manifest from fear. Further, the presence of the emotion of fear (not to be confused with the early warning signs of inner sensations) provides the opportunity to center attention on feeling rather than thoughts, allowing us to more easily digest the emotion. Obviously, this practice is necessary for if it were not, the emotion would not be present at all. Therefore, we can be grateful for the opportunity for the further development of expanded consciousness through the presence of disruptive emotions.

I am reminded of the first experience I had with mindfulness practice and noticing the subtle nature of the feeling state. Mindfulness, simply put, is paying attention to present moment sensations, feelings, and thoughts, non-judgmentally, with acceptance. During the practice, which was prescribed by the highly regarded mindfulness teacher Shinzen Young, I found feelings to be far subtler than thought and image, and even more so than the three outwardly directed focuses of attention of sight, sound, and touch. Once, when I was in the Contemplative Education class in grad school, I reached what seemed like a major breakthrough when I finally recognized the feeling space during meditation.

The feeling space (where both inner sensations and emotions arise) had been the most difficult for me to locate, as no feelings would surface while I was in such a restful state. In actuality, those underlying feelings may have been present all along only I simply needed more experience recognizing them. However, with practice, I began to notice the underlying fear beneath the level of thought. For example, the fear of not being able to complete grad school was present but I was unaware of it. To me, that was an indication that consciousness had expanded because in the past, I simply would not have even been aware of its presence.

With expanded consciousness comes greater understanding and acceptance of what is happening around us. According to Patanjali, "The enlightened do not overmuch grieve or rejoice in the changes of the relative Universe." In other words, those who are totally aware of the influence emotions play in their lives are likely to invest less energy in the highs and lows of life occurrences.

Once I was watching a basketball game and the local team was in a close game against a division rival. I thought of it as an "important" game and as I watched, I noticed when I would become emotionally charged and feel "good" when the home team was playing well and winning. However, as soon as they were not playing well (or at least their opponents were playing better), I suddenly had a different experience with the emotional charge. Now the interpretation of the feeling was "bad."

I began to wonder, did the energy I was experiencing within shift because of a basketball game? Not likely! It is more likely that either I mentally relabeled it, and there was really no shift at all, or the shift occurred in response to the thought of mentally re-labeling the feeling. In either case, the body was feeling energy and then contracted when the feeling was labeled as "bad" and expanded when labeled as "good."

As I was noticing this shift from pleasure to pain to pleasure again, I realized the absurdity of it all and let it go. Then I was able to watch the game without attachment to the results. This made for a more enjoyable experience. The game went into overtime and I was able to leave rather than stay to the end and perhaps commiserate on a "heartbreaking loss." Or, if the home team had won, celebrate excessively on a "hard fought win."

In either case, I would be fixating attention on the result of the changing ways of the world and most likely be increasing the mind's attachment to it. In so doing, I would be doomed to ride on the outside of the tornado of life and fight for survival amongst the myriad of objects caught up in the storm as well. Instead, I could choose to place attention on the center, or the eye of the storm in this analogy, and merely witness the objects swirling around and enjoy watching them dance. This is what it means to live life from the authentic rather than the psychological self.

CHAPTER 3

The Purpose of Emotional Pain

Now seems to be a good time to consider the purpose of pain. The purpose of outer pain is to protect the body and allow it to grow. For example, when we are young we don't have a grasp on how the body fits with the environment and we must learn through trial and error. If we touch something hot we will feel pain, causing us to move away, preventing the body from being damaged further. In turn, the body is allowed to grow in a natural progression through life. Hence, outer pain leads to outer growth.

Similarly, we undergo inner pain for inner growth. However, much like outer and inner are opposite ends of the spectrum to the concept of body, so to must we go in the opposite direction for growth when it comes to the inner world. In other words, typically, we must turn away from pain in the outer world to protect the body and allow it to grow. However, it's best to turn *toward* pain in the inner world to allow for growth.

Wayne Dyer wrote, "The painful events in our lives are like a raft you use to cross the river. You must remember to get off on the other side." This seems to indicate that we must be careful not to explain the present moment in terms of traumatic events of the past. It does not mean we should not deal with the trauma from the event. Indeed, we must deal with the distressing event and then move on.

Let's compare this with the healing of a physical wound. If the wound remains open, it can become infected and kill the entire organism. If it closes without being cleaned, it can still lead to infection and the same result might occur. Therefore, like properly cleaning a wound before covering it, we must look at the emotions as they occur and feel them fully, allowing the emotional charge to be released from the body. This is a good way to discover the truth beneath the feeling, or "the truth below your surface" as Dr. Dyer put it.

It seems that we can only get below the surface after that surface has been roughed up a great deal from some sort of traumatic life event. There are certainly plenty to choose from. When the surface gets roughed up by one of life's storms we must look deeper within ourselves to the calm waters residing beneath the level of the emotions. The problem is, once those waters have been smoothed out we stop looking beneath the surface until the next storm comes along.

The key is to deal with life's challenges as they occur and then let them go. How much mental energy do we use up thinking of past events that cannot change? We need only acknowledge these thoughts as they enter the mind, take heed of the lesson, and move the focus of attention to present moment thinking. "Don't think about it," is the wrong advice. One must acknowledge the thought to avoid repeating the error in the future. However, one must not *keep* thinking about it.

The Buddha once said, "When touched with a feeling of pain the ordinary person laments…becomes distraught…contracts…so he feels two pains…just as if they were to shoot a man with an arrow

28

and, right afterward, were to shoot him with another…so that he would feel the pains of two arrows…" In the experience I have had with digesting emotions, if we center awareness on the feeling as it arises, without thinking about why it is there, we will avoid the pain of the "second arrow" because we will not be "lamenting" over the original emotional pain.

It helps to remember that we make ourselves unhappy because of thoughts we have about circumstances in life. People don't make us unhappy. We only become unhappy after first having a thought about what others are doing and *may* be thinking. It is helpful to ask ourselves, "Is this feeling of anger (or depression, guilt, etc.) going to produce the results I want?" If the answer is no (and it almost always is outside the present moment), we can change the thought and we will change the feeling or emotion associated with it.

It is okay to use an angry look or voice to get a response as long as we do not internalize it. If our child is running out in the middle of the street, for example, we might want to use a loud "angry" voice to get the child to stop immediately. If that is the intention of using the angry voice then it is healthy, as long as we do not internalize it. We internalize it by continuing to ruminate on it and by identifying with the behavior, either our child's or ours. For example, we might think, *my* child is irresponsible. I must watch him closely so he doesn't hurt himself. Or, we might think, I am an angry parent. In either case, rather than seeing the behavior as something that occurred in that moment, we begin to define our "self," or the self of the child, as one who *is* the behavior.

It is helpful to remember that, like thoughts, the emotions are not us. If this is true, then what are they? Thoughts and emotions are part of a guidance system that can lead us to increased levels of consciousness, often referred to as "spirit," or the breath of life. It is the formless life energy that permeates form. It is beneath the level of thought and emotion, the one that is aware of both. The more we can separate ourselves from thought and emotion, the more "in spirit" we are, which is to say, the more we are operating from a higher level of consciousness.

Thought and emotion can be conceptualized as the connection or link between the mind/body of the physical plane of existence and the formless life energy of consciousness in the nonphysical plane. One reason we tend to confuse the mind/body complex (or ego) with consciousness is it is not of a physical nature, that is to say, we are involved in it but we cannot see it.

Thought appears to be a part of the no thing world, or the "spirit world," as it is so often described. This is the world of no form. It is the world of energy, consciousness. Similarly, the emotional reaction within the body also appears to have no form and therefore, it seems to belong in the realm of spirit as well. In this way it is easy to see why we might come to believe that we are the thoughts and emotions. They are more intimate than the body. Indeed, others can see the body we are housed in but can they see the mind? Can they see what we are feeling if it is not written all over our face?

It is the role of the thought/emotion phenomenon that makes it so difficult to discern between it and consciousness. Since its role is to act as a conduit between the physical and nonphysical world, the observable difference between them is subtle. Only when we can accept that thoughts and emotions are a function of consciousness rather than consciousness itself, can we truly perceive consciousness in its purest sense, which is unbounded and infinite.

CHAPTER 4

Don't Take Yourself Too Seriously

Before moving on, it is important to discern how feelings are turned into emotions in the first place. If the feeling we are experiencing is simply energy flowing through the body, then why do we attach meaning to it and label it as anger, fear, resentment, sadness, guilt or the multitude of other disruptive emotions, alongside the pleasant emotions of excited, happy, joyous, etc.? The answer to this question is really quite simple. We attach meaning to the different emotions so that we can remember whether or not we liked the outcome associated with our actions.

If we act in a way that causes conflict between another and our "self," it is important to remember what we did so that we can learn from our error and keep from making the same mistake in the future. For example, we might judge another person for failing to act in a way we perceive as appropriate for any given situation, causing him or her to respond harshly to us, creating an emotional charge. Then, the mind begins sending thoughts attempting to explain the meaning of the feeling. It might say, "I shouldn't have said that, I hurt her feelings. I should apologize." Or it might say, "I don't know what he is getting so upset about. I didn't say anything wrong. He shouldn't be so sensitive." In either case the mind is trying to send us thoughts to explain why the person reacted in that way. Again, these thoughts are neither good or bad, or right or wrong. They are just thoughts. Therefore, it is important not to give them too much stock.

One way to look at the type of incident described above is when an emotional episode occurs; we can say a friendly hello to the non-friendly ego, the egoic part of us causing the disturbance in the body. What we are doing is sending high frequency thoughts (often labeled as positive) to the lower frequency thoughts (typically labeled as negative), and the emotional episode is likely to lose much of its power. This is why it is helpful to not take the self too seriously.

Once several years ago, I was talking to my daughter "A" about how I had been learning to quiet the mind and how much I enjoyed the experience. She listened intently while I shared the story with her. Then she said, "Dad. That was the most boring story in the history of boring stories!" It was so funny I laughed out loud! This is a great example of the importance of not taking oneself too seriously. Had I taken myself too seriously, the ego would have run the show and there may have been conflict. However, as it turned out, A and I shared a good laugh together.

I am reminded of the scene from the movie *Anger Management*, in which the main character (portrayed by Adam Sandler) went to talk to a former classmate he harbored ill feelings toward. This former acquaintance had become a monk and was living in a monastery. The monk tried hard to maintain a peace filled heart but finally caved as a result of being continually badgered by his old nemesis, who he used to bully when they were kids. This was a rather humorous way of demonstrating the difficulty of maintaining our inner peace in the presence of hostility.

It must be remembered that learning to digest emotions in the present moment may not always be easy. In the story above, the monk attempted to turn his attention to his center but each attempt was thwarted by Sandler's character, intentionally trying to disrupt his peace. However, the disruption of peace does not always have to be intentional.

Once while in graduate school I was preparing to take a test in statistics. I could feel an emotional charge as the time to begin approached so I turned attention directly to it. I "shined a light of healing on it" as a good friend put it. However, later while taking the test the thought crossed the mind that I had made a crucial mistake. I thought I had run the wrong analysis on the first problem, thereby crippling me for the rest of the test. The thought seemed to have a strong enough effect to disrupt the ability to perform on the remainder of the exam. As it turned out, I actually ran the initial analysis correctly. However, the erroneous thinking led to me running the following two analyses incorrectly. This incident had a profound effect on me, allowing me to realize just how disruptive even erroneous thoughts can be.

On another day I was walking with a friend and she told me she mentally shut down. When I inquired as to why, she said it was because I had failed to give attention to the poster she wanted to show me, and, in fact, I had even groaned about it. I could tell it was her ego but at the same time, the ego in me got activated. I could feel it all over the body. As I attempted to turn attention toward it, the friend I was with tried continually to get me to interact with her.

Upon reflection, I realized that this is the type of behavior that leads to many arguments. As attention is drawn away from the inner feeling (like it did for me in both examples above), we tend to forget about it and immediately get drawn into the content of mind. The moment we do that emotion runs free, attention goes toward the cause of the aroused state, and suddenly we are drawn into an ego war. However, with practice, we can become more adept at maintaining at least a portion of attention on the inner feelings and allow them to dissipate, while at the same time, listen intently to what the other person has to say. In turn, the emotional "pain" occurring can actually help us to become more present in the moment.

In order to turn attention to the emotion, however, we must discover our "feeling space." The feeling space is the place where emotions tend to arise and may be different for everyone. For me, the feeling space is located in the solar plexus, or just above the belly button deep in the body, right around where the lumbar and thoracic vertebrae come together.

After discovering this place I seemed to undergo a shift in consciousness. It is a very difficult thing to put to words but I will do the best I can. Once, several years ago I noticed that when events occurred that previously had elicited an emotional charge, suddenly there was none. I would notice the trigger, automatically turn attention toward the feel space in which it typically arose, and simply observe it. Nothing would happen. Then, after a brief pause, the mind would start up again and from the stillness would come the thought, "Nope, I guess not."

So what was the shift? It appears I became aware of the location when attending to the feel space. Moreover, attention seemed to go there automatically without having to direct it through personal volition. Further, when there was an emotional charge it seemed milder, perhaps due to a more definitive nonjudgmental acceptance of the feeling. However, when I did react to the trigger, although the feeling was not as strong as in the past, the tone in the voice was still the same.

Interestingly, the vocal tone was stronger than the feeling itself, which is the complete opposite of what I had experienced before that time. Indeed, I can recall repressing the words, and in so doing, repress the anger as well. Unfortunately, when we repress angry emotions they typically get expressed in another way and often times they are misdirected, as described earlier. I was then able to use that mental shift and newfound sensitivity to subtle emotions advantageously in everyday life. For example, one morning a former girlfriend, who I will refer to as B, said that I could, "feel free to consider doing the dishes" in a rather sarcastic way.

I immediately responded, "Okay B," with tone in the voice. This was an obvious indication that her comment angered me. However, when attention was spontaneously drawn to the feeling there was very little to be found. I now had a decision to make, to do the dishes or not. The big question to me became to what thoughts and emotions would I be acting on? Would I be choosing to not do the dishes to spite B? Or, perhaps I would choose to do the dishes to make her feel guilty about her comment.

Obviously, I didn't want to choose from either of those places. Upon recognizing this, I chose to clean the kitchen knowing that B had already done her share and would most likely be cooking breakfast later that morning. This was coming from the place of love rather than the place of fear. I say fear rather than anger because anger seems to be a specific type of fear. In this case, the anger was really coming from the idea that I might be seen as a selfish, non-giving person who does not do his fair share of the work, hence, fear.

When I first began the practice of noticing and accepting emotions as they arose it was superficial at best. The thought of accept the emotion was there, but the *feeling* of acceptance was missing. In other words, although I told myself to accept it, there was still a large part of me that would say, "I don't want to feel this way!" Fortunately however, the thought began to be followed with another, namely, "...so I better keep practicing." In this way, the feeling was turned into motivation and utilized to get what I wanted, rather than what I *thought* I wanted, which was for the feeling to go away. What I *really* wanted was to be free from the bondage of the ego.

It is helpful to remember, however, that to be free of the ego is not to say we will no longer experience feelings. Feelings serve an important function. They alert us to be present. Typically we don't become present however; rather, attention gets pulled into thought. Then we are no longer in the present moment. Instead, we are lost in

37

thought. In turn, our decision-making becomes weakened as it is swayed by memories of past experiences.

This is not to say that memories of past experiences don't serve a purpose; they do! However, the purpose they serve, which is to help guide us in future experiences, becomes obscured because we fail to see (or remember) that these thoughts and feelings are from the past. In turn, our decision to act is often times more influenced by the past than the present. In contrast, if we are grounded in the present moment, when thoughts and emotions from the past do arise we can notice them, be still, and become alert to what is happening now. Then we can act from this place of stillness. In turn, we can make a high quality decision based on the current situation, while at the same time, be informed by past experience.

I am reminded of a story of a certain disciple who asked his teacher how to enter Zen. The teacher responded with a question of his own. He asked, "Do you hear the sound of the creek in the distance?"

At first the student did not hear the creek because he was so consumed with thoughts of learning the art of Zen. After becoming very still and listening with high alertness, however, he heard the faint sound of water in the distance. When the student told the master he heard it the master's response was, "Enter Zen from there."

After pausing for a moment and reflecting on the teaching the student asked, "Master, what would you have said if I said I didn't hear it?"

To which the master replied, "Enter Zen from there."

In other words, we enter Zen, or present moment awareness, by being still. It is in the silent pause where we will find truth. It is the place where the authentic self resides, uninhibited by the socially constructed self. Further, we must begin practicing being present from wherever we are in the current moment. Some will have more egoic tendencies built up that need noticed and released. Others may have very little to process. In either case, we are being told to begin practice from the place that applies to us.

It is also helpful to remember that letting go of ego is not the same as forgetting about and ignoring past experience; rather, it is about letting go of the emotional charge associated with the memory so that present moment decisions are not clouded by it. In order to do that, we must learn to become the witness of the emotions, as will be discussed in the next chapter.

CHAPTER 5

Be the Witness of the Emotion

Carl Jung once said, "As with all dangers, we can guard against the risk of psychic infection only when we know what is attacking us, and how, where, and when the attack will come." Therefore, we must learn to become more aware of the emotions when they arise so that we can watch them non-judgmentally. That is what it means to be the witness of the emotion. We watch it without reacting to it.

Swami Kriyananda, a disciple of Paramahansa Yogananda writes, "Pure reason and pure feeling are both intuitive; but when reason is circumscribed by the intellectuality of the sense-bound mind, and feeling devolves into egoistic emotion, these instrumentalities of the soul produce distorted perceptions." He goes on to write, "But when chitta – human knowing and feeling – is calmed by meditation, the ordinary agitated ego gives way to the blessed calmness of soul perception."

It seems the authentic self is attempting to pull awareness into the present moment and the psychological self is trying to pull it into past/future thinking, thereby creating tension. This is reminiscent of the psychological concept of cognitive dissonance, which is when a person holds two incongruous ideas simultaneously, creating psychological tension. For example, if a person enjoys smoking but believes it to be unhealthy, the decision to continue smoking may create a tension in the body. This is where stress comes from.

I find it fascinating that we are made of 99.99% space yet we live in the .01 percent most of the time. Indeed, science tells us that, despite appearances, everything in the physical world is actually nothing more than vibrating energy. It has been posited that if we were to blow up an atom to the size of a domed stadium and placed a BB at midfield to represent the nucleus, the electrons would be nothing more than ghosts flickering in and out of existence in the nose bleed seats of the arena. Everything else is empty space!

Despite this understanding, we get wrapped up in the contractions of the body and lose sight of our center, which is, coincidently, the space of that other 99.99%. If we can reside in the space instead of the contraction we remain centered and will be at peace always. Merely be in the space when the contraction occurs, that is to say, be the witness of it. Then stay there by continuing to watch it until it dissipates.

Being the witness of the emotions as they occur is something like sitting and intentionally contracting and relaxing our stomach muscles. When we do it consciously we are the witness of it. Believe it or not, we can do the exact same thing with emotions. Just witness them without attempting to figure out why they are there. However, we must train ourselves to do that.

Observing our self experience the emotion is one way to diffuse the physiological effects of that emotion. One such example of this occurred one day while being involved in a lockdown drill at school. Apparently I had failed to lock one of the doors, as a police officer was able to open it and peer inside. What he saw was the entire class lined up in a row against the wall like sitting ducks. Several thoughts began to pour through the mind. I thought about the embarrassment I would feel later as the staff was being debriefed. I kept thinking to myself, how could you not lock that door?

Earlier I had checked the door from the inside and it felt locked. However, I did not open the door and check from the outside, which is a pretty simple mistake. In addition, in previous experience that particular door had *always* been locked. Moreover, there are many doors to check in the lower gym so I suppose it would be rather easy to miss one.

As all these thoughts raced through the mind I sat there, dumbfounded. Another person opened the door and looked inside. After the thought of *we're dead* had worn off, I decided that we, in fact, were not dead and in a real emergency I would simply correct the error and go lock the door. After all, it may have been a student looking to get in out of the hall. So that is the action I took. Taking this action helped to make me feel a little better.

I went back to sit down with the students and started a conversation with myself. I started to look for the good that could come from all this. The thought occurred to me, it is a good thing this happened because now I won't let it happen in a *real* emergency. It was at that time an amazing thing happened. As I focused on the good that would come from this uncomfortable event, the internal strife simply vanished. This is the power of changing our focus to what good can come from each situation. It changes our perspective from loss to gain.

In the psychology literature, the idea presented above is referred to as cognitive reframing. This simply means to attempt to re-perceive the event and see it in a new light. We can do this in each and every situation we find ourselves in that elicits a disruptive emotional response. All we must do is search for what good can come from each event. At times it may require zooming out and looking at the big picture. However, during personal experience there has *always* been something good that can come from each incident. Indeed, it appears to me that every life event carries the purpose of inner growth. However, in order to grow from the event we must face it head on rather than turn away from it.

Philosopher Alfred Korsyvski stated, "Anything you know about cannot be you." The incident discussed above demonstrated to me that the more I witnessed the emotional charge present in the body, the more I recognized it was not me. In turn, the easier it became to be separate from it and act independent of it. I no longer asked myself why I felt this way. Instead, I asked what belief must I let go of in order to feel at peace.

Becoming the witness of thoughts and emotions is the way to peace. This idea has been termed "quantum observation" by Stephen Wolinsky in his book titled *Quantum Consciousness*. To me, the key to this quantum observation appears to be eliminating all judgment. However, it can pose quite a challenge because much of the ego is hidden from us. Indeed, according to Meher Baba, "The ego is like an iceberg. Ninety percent of it is under water. As we observe it the submerged begins to move into the light of observation, and melts in the light of awareness." This is what we are able to do when we look upon emotions non-judgmentally.

Wolinsky suggested that the difference between a "dissociator" and a "merger" is crucial when it comes to quantum observation. According to the author, a dissociator is one who dissociates from the feeling and is on the opposite end of the spectrum from one who merges with the feeling. Neither however is truly free, as the first cannot tolerate the feeling and the second cannot free himself from it. This is yet another example of finding the middle way, where one is neither intolerant of the feeling nor lost in it. This is also why it is important to ride the wave of the emotion and let it run its course, without repressing it or wishing it was not there. In turn, we can we become free of it.

Similarly, with thoughts we must simply observe them, find the gap between them and settle there. A good analogy to go along with this concept is how a surfer watches the waves before finding the sweet spot between them. She then rides comfortably in that place of calm and feels exhilarated by the freedom. This is much like meditation where we try to find that place of calm peace between the thoughts.

"By allowing the natural, outward motion of energy to occur, the energy passes right through you. In essence, you can get out of the way and allow the energy to do what it does." This quote by Wolinsky seems to epitomize the experience I have had in feeling the energy of the emotion while it occurs rather than begin to think about what it means. More often than not, the energy does seem to pass right through me. I am then free to act in whatever way will serve me best.

Wolinsky went on to write, "Only when we experience these intense states do we begin to dissipate the charge from the emotion." Several years ago a good friend of mine told me that a rumor of me drinking at a summer camp was running through the community in which I coached basketball. Parent volunteers were supervising the players and I was not needed. However, the thought of the head coach going out drinking with other coaches didn't sit well with some of the parents. Consequently, I experienced some extremely powerful emotions.

In the past I may have decided to have a few drinks to calm the nerves. However, on this occasion I wanted to feel the feelings fully so I consciously decided to abstain from drinking while doing just that. For two days I stayed home by myself and felt the emotions without wishing them away. I simply stayed on the couch and let them flow.

The mind was feeding the body all kinds of thoughts about how embarrassed I would be to face members of the community, and how I might lose the coaching job over this, and what co-workers, friends, and family might think if I did lose the coaching position. Each time a thought like this would occur, another wave of emotion would flood the body. However, as described in the paragraphs above, I simply rode the wave of the emotion until it dissipated, like a wave rolling back into the sea.

After this rather humbling event I came to recognize the truth behind the emotions being energy we have labeled with past experiences. We remember events similar to the one we are experiencing, similar emotions are stirred (which we have labeled as fear, anxiety, anger, etc.), and the mind picks the one that seems most fitting for the given situation. Once we become accustomed to experiencing the emotional charge without labeling it or attempting to explain it or wish it away, the energy passes through the body uninhibited.

CHAPTER 6

What Is, Is

In *The Second Book of the Tao*, Stephen Mitchell states, "Though we actually live in what is, we think ourselves into what isn't." This quote was in response to the Tao, or the way things are. It is helpful to remember that thought is nothing more than a tape recorder of our past history, reformatted to try to explain the present moment. The problem is the present moment can no more be explained by past events than awareness can be explained by thought. Awareness can only be known by letting go of thought. Hence, awareness can only be practiced. It cannot be described because it would be described by what it isn't. This seems to be the ultimate paradox.

According to Mitchell, "Life becomes very gentle when you understand that you're not living it." He went on to write that the theory of everything may as well be "what is, is." It is as simple as that. Instead of striving for perfection, all we need do is be, and then accept what is. We cannot change what reality has set forth; we can only adjust the path we walk along with it. Moreover, if we make no adjustments and simply walk the path laid before us, all we need do is breath. Everything else will take care of itself.

What is perfection? What is! The only thing that is perfect is reality. Most of us compare reality with what we would like it to be to be perfect. But how can reality be less than perfect? It is what it is and nothing changes that. How can that be less than perfect? How do

47

we know reality is perfect? Because it is! How does it get any simpler than that?

Suffering only occurs when we want things to be different than they are. In essence, this puts us at odds with reality and creates tension in the mind (i.e., suffering). There is no suffering in the eternal now. When we are totally present there is only action and no action. Perhaps that may even be a misnomer, as *action* is perceived in the physical world only, which according to science, is an optical illusion. Things happen, awareness witnesses it, and then more things happen. In reality, there is not a doer doing anything. There is only consciousness experiencing the change of form.

There is no need for mental suffering. Sure, it might provide guilt, which could lead us to choose right action, but it seems to me that it took getting lost in thought in the first place that led us to act in a way that caused us to feel guilty. In contrast, if we were always in the now, right action would spontaneously arise out of that place when required. And what is "right action?" Right action is whatever happens in the now, with non-judgment about what is happening, and with non-attachment to the outcome. This is the place of no mind. It is the place where we accept what is, for no other reason than it is the way things are. Again, we must let life lead the way, because it does anyway, with or without our permission or our acceptance. If we fight with reality, we lose!

Some would say this is living in a dream, as there is no way a person could live in a world without suffering. Typically, people with this perspective also say that to suffer can be a "good" thing because it demonstrates caring for self and others. However, this is merely an illusion. To suffer does not indicate caring, rather, it indicates ignorance to the reality that there is no need to suffer and nothing good can come from it. Indeed, if a person fell in a well would it benefit him for us to jump in with him? Of course not! We could attempt to help him out of the well, but to join him in the hole would simply add to the suffering. Similarly, if a person is feeling stressed and expressing his displeasure to us, if we join in on the complaining we simply perpetuate his suffering.

I want to point out that experiencing disruptive emotions is *not* suffering. It is the resisting of those emotions that leads to suffering. Experiencing them with acceptance is not painful, especially if we are able to watch the emotions with curiosity. Indeed, they can be quite interesting. If someone says that I am delusional and living in a dream world, why would I listen? Why would I want to join them in their dream? If they are feeling combative with this type of dream, what must theirs be like?

It seems that when we are attached to the outcome of any event the body is in a state of tension, almost bracing for the fall. This is what happens when we project ourselves to the future rather than stay grounded in the now. It is also what happens when we are fixated on the past, such as when we feel guilt, regret, or shame. In either case, because we are arguing with what is, we suffer.

Once a few years ago the thought occurred to me that I had to go out in the backyard and fold up a big tarp I had laid there to dry, as I didn't want it to damage the grass. Instantly I felt a sharp pain course through the midsection, indicating I did not want to follow through with the thought. I felt it immediately and recognized at once I was fighting with reality. I then simply let go of the feeling by intentionally relaxing the area and half laughed at the ego that wanted to take me down the path of suffering, even over something as trivial as putting away a tarp.

The incident described above reminded me of a quote I read attributed to Chuang Tzu, a highly regarded teacher of Taoism from some 2,300 years ago, who wrote, "The master examines his innermost self. He notices even the smallest sign of discord, and corrects it before it can do any harm." Had I not recognized the feeling for what it was, I no doubt would have been led to a place I did not want to go. Instead, I was able to laugh at the self and remain in a state of peace. Then, from that place, I went out and folded up the tarp.

If we can always remember to be the witness of thoughts and emotions we can be free of them. That is what it means to be liberated from the ego. Perhaps this is what it truly means to be "saved." We are saved from the torture of the ego or "hell." How does the ego create hell on earth? By collecting the energy from past events and then unconsciously spewing it out on whoever meets the criteria. What are the right criteria? The right triggers. This is why siblings are good at "pulling our strings" or "pushing our buttons," as are our partners. The closer we become to someone, the more likely they will know our triggers. Of course, if they go for the trigger it is their ego that chooses to pull it. Why? Because it needs to be fed with more energy. However, I must add here that our loved ones are not always triggering us on purpose. They just happen to push the right buttons, which may be why they are in our life in the first place.

Csikszentmihalyi quoted Edmund Burke who wrote, "He who wrestles with us strengthens our nerves, and sharpens our skill. Our antagonist is our helper." This quote supports what I am suggesting above, namely, that our siblings, along with those who are close to us, play a vital role in our psychological development by helping us notice any stored emotional energy, thereby providing us with the opportunity to release it.

Emotions are extremely important in that they help us relate to others. However, when seen through the veil of the ego, the individual becomes misguided. People can be triggers. There is no doubt about it. We can find peace by choosing to avoid those triggers by being reclusive. And many people decide to do just that. However, there is another way. We can interact with people with more awareness, realizing that if they trigger an emotional reaction in us it provides us with an opportunity. Once the emotion has been exposed it can be looked at, fully felt, and released. This is what it means to "exorcise the demons." The so-called "demons" are remembered thoughts that dig up stored emotions from our personal history, and to exorcise them means feel and release them. Once that is done it is done, and the more we practice digesting the emotions the less we have to release.

So, how do we avoid the trigger trap? It is helpful to keep

awareness centered on the core body. That way, if an emotion were to arise, it can be felt before it reaches the thought. In contrast, if the awareness is already in thought, the energy from the emotion any given thought triggers (and eventually one will be found) will not be noticed. In turn, we would come from the place of the ego. We would be acting as if each thought were true.

Have you ever noticed how many thoughts are meaningless repeated phrases over and over? Few of them are necessary. And few of them are true, at least absolutely. In fact, in terms of absolute truth, no thought could be that. This is because the thought takes a piece of the whole by its very nature. To explain an event we must take it out of a series of another, and that from a series of another, and another, and so on and so forth. Therefore, there is no way a thought can be an absolute truth, including the one expressed in this very sentence. How is that for a paradox?

Ironically, what I wrote above (along with the help of the woman I was dating at the time) inspired me to stop attempting to speak in absolute terms. There is only one absolute. It is what is referred to as "God." This is why so many spiritual and religious teachings suggest that God cannot be spoken of. It's the one absolute. Interestingly, this is also why terms such as these are often capitalized in spiritual literature.

The ego is like an energy vampire feeding on the energy of other egos. This is why people send sarcastic jokes toward others. Their ego is attempting to stir the ego in the other in the hopes of sucking its energy and building upon its sense of self. Is it any wonder why ego is often referred to as self? For example, let's say a student calls out another student from across the room by sending out a "friendly" jibe. High school boys are notorious for this. His ego is attempting to build its self at the expense of another.

When it does so, all the egos of those sitting near enough to hear become active. Then the instigator has nearby energy to suck. Those who feel uncomfortable at the jibe have their energy sucked by those who find it funny. So now, both the instigator and those who found it funny have reinforced their own egos, at the expense of others. Moreover, those who gained egoic energy will now be forced to face more drama in their lives. It will eventually stir the ego in others and create an altercation. This is the true meaning of karma. And it happens all the time.

Paradoxically, the "victims" in this situation, the ones who surrendered egoic energy by having compassion for the other, will actually be the "winners." Why? Because they released the egoic energy to the vampires, they will incur less drama through altercations with others. They have simply accrued less karma. In fact, they have actually released some karma from past events.

However, there is a twist. Those who continue to feel bad for the other do not surrender their psychic energy. Rather, they hold onto it and find something to attach it to, like perhaps the idea that the world is a hostile and dangerous place. They then become fearful and avoid interacting with others. In this case, they actually reinforce their own ego by holding in the energy that was stirred. In contrast, those who feel inspired enough to go over and help the other, the one

53

who received the initial barb that started this whole chain reaction in the first place, can transform the egoic energy into love energy by lifting the other up and helping him to feel better.

In this situation, both individuals undergo a growth of consciousness, creating less space to be occupied by egoic energy. In turn, less karma accrued and less drama lay ahead, for that is the way that it works. As consciousness expands there is less room for the "psychic energy" as Jung would put it, to form and hence, the ego in the individual(s) has been reduced.

One of the most profound experiences I have had with regards to digesting emotions and letting go came after ending a three-year relationship with B, whom I dated throughout most of grad school. By the time we separated I had been practicing processing emotions in the way discussed earlier, that is to say, by turning attention to them fully without attempting to analyze them. Interestingly, I read about the stages of death (denial, anger, bargaining, depression and acceptance) not long after we separated and the comparison was obvious.

In his book, *Further Along the Road Less Traveled,* Scott Peck suggested we go through these stages in all of life's big events that lead to growth, assuming we are able to go through all of them. I had heard this before but reading it at that time in life, when I was in the process of working through the loss of the relationship, was profound to say the least.

Although I was in agreement when we broke off the relationship, as I reflected on all the good times we shared, I began to question the decision. First I denied the reality, saying to myself, "It's just comps. When she finishes her exams we will have an opportunity to work through it." I stayed in that stage until the day she completed the exams. That night I received some text messages that seemed quite similar to the ones she sent when she was in DC and found herself attracted to another man.

The next day the hunch (not to be confused with intuition) was confirmed when she told me she *was* with another man at the time of the texts and they had shared their feelings for one another. This information moved me out of denial and into anger. I was angry with the other guy and had thoughts of retribution. I was angry with myself and had thoughts of regret. I was angry with B and had thoughts of never speaking to her again, and telling her how much she hurt me and that she would come to regret it.

After walking around the neighborhood, however, I moved out of the anger stage and into bargaining. The thought occurred to me that perhaps there is still a chance. Perhaps I could talk to her and we could work things out. Actually I had gone through these stages as she was preparing for the exams and went back through them again upon hearing the news of her having feelings for someone else.

After returning from the walk I moved into the stage of depression. However, I knew at the time that all I need do was continue to feel the feelings to move through this stage and into acceptance. Then I could experience the growth associated with accepting this loss. Interestingly, I could see how accepting the subjective *and* objective loss of the relationship with B would allow

55

for inner growth. I say subjective because of the thoughts associated with the meaning of the relationship, and objective because of the physical realities of physical touch and closeness as well as the living situation (we had been living together for most of those three years while in a relationship). With these "things" out of the way, more conscious awareness was allowed to shine through.

Amazingly, the thought mentioned above coincided with thoughts that occurred to me on a commute to the city the day before. The idea was that as less conscious awareness is directed to subjective reality (i.e., thoughts), and objective reality (i.e., traffic), space consciousness grows. In turn, we tend to find more peace, both in our subjective and objective experience. In the case of traffic, for example, as I turned attention to the space in front of me the thoughts slowed down and I found more subjective peace. In addition, the more I turned attention to the space, the more space that was created between myself and the other cars on the road. In the case of accepting the end of the relationship, because of the years practicing digesting emotions, I was able to go through the final four stages of death (in this case loss) in a matter of minutes.

CHAPTER 7

Acceptance of Emotions

An important aspect of digesting emotions is the art of total non-resistance. With regards to emotions, the total allowance of them seems to dissolve them. What does that mean? It means whatever feeling arises we must make friends with it. As described earlier, we just turn all attention to the energy flowing through the body and label it "feeling," which is a word that does not connote good or bad. We come from the place, where we say its okay, I'll allow it, and then simply observe what happens. If we continue with this practice the mind begins to select different thoughts, perhaps as a means of getting us to face whatever previous emotions we stored rather than released during the original emotional episode.

Only here's where it can get tricky. If we direct our emotional charge at another individual they will typically do one of three things, they will either, store it themselves and hold a grudge against us, allow it to pass on by, or they will send it back to us, plus the bonus of added energy they release from their own previously formed ego self. Some would describe this as karma. I like to think of it as instant karma and we are fortunate to get a chance to try again. If we can then recognize the ego in us and accept it as okay, then we will be free to let it go. It seems quite paradoxical.

Typically, what happens next is we may be able to sincerely apologize and accept responsibility for our actions. After all, the part that arose in us *is* our responsibility. If we say otherwise we are choosing to be the victim. In order to remain in a state of peace, we must completely accept what happens to us, at least that which has already occurred. This by all means does not mean that we cannot then move away from that which can harm us physically. It is speaking internally; how we react to the event. Do we lash out at another? Do we deny it? Do we suggest to ourselves it isn't real and thereby suppress it? Or, do we totally feel it and accept it? If we continue to attempt to do the latter, we will soon become experts at digesting emotions, because life will provide all the opportunities we need, guaranteed!

Perhaps when we have come to accept everything that is, we will no longer face trials and tribulations. Life will always be peaceful. Until then, emotionally arousing events will continue to keep happening. However, as long as we observe them nonjudgmentally, we will eventually come to a point that the mind will no longer label them at all. In turn, our relation to the events will change. No longer will the body contract in response to the event. To me, this is what it means to be "enlightened." Although physical reality may not change, our relation to it does.

Similar to watching emotions, it is equally as important to watch thoughts. We can notice them, label them as "talk," and accept them as okay. We just don't act on them right away. We can simply open awareness to the entire environment, including our internal self or ego, and the right path will reveal itself. If we can choose from this place of stillness, then we can act independent of the psychological self. Only then can we find truth. After all, who would think the ego would direct us to truth? It's absurd!

It is helpful to remember that when we are children, our parents and society condition our psychological self, both intentionally and unintentionally. Some of this conditioning may serve a valuable purpose, such as how we can understand and get along with others. However, much of it will no longer serve us. Then we will need to de-condition the mind to the same extent it was conditioned. Some have done it all at once, perhaps through complete acceptance of a traumatic life event. Others take much longer, and they must face many small frustrations and release each one individually as they arise.

Another aspect to consider about digesting emotions is the influence metacognition has on our emotional state. Metacognition is, simply put, thinking about thinking. When we first begin to practice being present, it is possible to become upset about finding ourselves lost in thought. We might begin to say to ourselves, "I'm no good at this!" or "I can't seem to get out of thought at all!" or something to that effect. This can be very damaging to our practice as it might cause us to lose motivation or even give up the practice altogether.

Instead of becoming upset about it, it is helpful to view it as a success. Indeed, every time we notice we are lost in thought *is* a moment to celebrate because it means we are becoming more aware. That is exactly why we are practicing! Therefore, when we notice that we are lost in thought, and we notice that the act of observing it creates an emotional charge, we can simply say to ourselves, "That's okay, it's good that I noticed it." Further, we can now congratulate ourselves on two levels. Not only did we notice we were lost in thought, but we also recognized the emotion that arose when observing it. Now we have two reasons to celebrate!

Similar to metacognition, we may come across meta-emotions when beginning to practice digesting them, that is to say, becoming emotional about experiencing emotions. For example, let's say that someone makes a comment that elicits an emotional charge and we become angry. Then, because we are practicing being present in part to find inner peace, we get angry with ourselves for becoming angry. This too can be damaging to our practice because it adds another layer of ego that must be penetrated in order to come from the place of the authentic self.

Therefore, it is helpful to acknowledge success when noticing a disruptive state. If an individual makes a comment that elicits an emotional charge in us and we notice the reaction, after first labeling it "feeling" as discussed earlier, we can then say to ourselves, "Good job noticing it!" or "This is good practice!" or some other congratulatory phrase. It is the acceptance of the disruptive state that transforms it. Indeed, how can one remain in a disturbed state while acknowledging success?

At times meta-emotions can work in the opposite way and keep us from experiencing joy in life. For example, we might be feeling especially fun loving one day and begin acting "goofy" in public as a means of being playful with a loved one. However, the mind might then say, "Don't act that way in public. You will make a fool of you self!" Then an emotion may arise that keeps us from acting in this playful manner. Where did that emotion come from? Perhaps when we were children and we were acting age appropriate our parent said to us, "Don't act that way in public. You are embarrassing me!" Then the chastising created a feeling of shame that we repressed, causing us to be much more reserved in the future. This is not to say that parents should not teach their kids appropriate behavior when in public. That is an important role for parents and it is helpful for them to do so. Rather, it is a way to recognize where our belief system came from so that we can now choose, as adults, which behaviors serve us best.

One way to rid ourselves of repressive thoughts and emotions derived from childhood is to intentionally place ourselves in situations that we know will offer us the opportunity to digest the emotions when they arise. For example, we can attempt to be less reserved and act goofy in public, knowing all along that part of the mind will be saying, "Don't act that way! You are too mature to behave in that manner." Then, when the emotion arises, we will be fully prepared to direct attention to it rather than to the thought that created it. This can prove to be a wonderful practice when it comes to shedding one's ego.

A good example of what I am referring to above is the act of skipping in public. How often do you see adults skip in public? I would guess it is rarely, if ever. Now ask yourself the question, why do children skip? The answer is simple, because it feels good.

I remember skipping with A in public when she was a little girl. At times it would elicit some odd looks from people but it didn't bother me because I was with A. Because of this practice, I remembered how good it felt to skip. However, when A was not with me I dared not to partake in that particular behavior. Why? The reason was social conditioning. I remembered hearing that adults don't do that sort of thing, and as an adult, I accepted that into the socially instilled belief system.

However, at one point, I decided to eliminate this limiting belief. After all, if I feel like skipping, or galloping, or prancing down the sidewalk for a few steps, what difference does it make if strangers think I am weird? And, as I mentioned earlier, I found it to be a good practice in digesting emotions. More importantly, it felt really good! Because of that I still often find myself doing a few quick shuttle steps while on a walk, regardless of whether anyone else is there to see it. Each and every time I feel a subtle charge of energy that feels good. It seems this is the reason animals behave in this way in nature, such as when we see antelope bounding around for no particular reason. It is merely a way to celebrate life, and it feels good.

As mentioned, accepting emotions is extremely important when it comes to digesting them. However, sometimes accepting the emotions just doesn't seem possible. If we cannot accept what we are currently doing we would be better off not doing it. Consider why we choose hobbies. When we choose a hobby it is typically because it helps us to be present. What do we find in that presence?

Often times it is joy and enthusiasm. It is a feeling of expansion. This is a key difference between what we consider to be work and play.

Why do we call one thing work and another play? When we think of work it is typically something we consider we "have" to do, such as we have to go to work to pay the bills. Once we make enough money to pay the bills, now we *get* to go out and "play," such as when we go on vacation, or when we use some of the work money to buy a camper or a boat or similar large adult toy that we can use on the weekend.

There are many different kinds of doing but here I would like to focus on just three, joyful, acceptant, and resentful. These three states are along a continuum of active doing, with joyful being at the end that feels the most expansive, resentful being at the end that feels the most contractive, and acceptant being somewhere in between. Typically, when we are choosing a hobby we are in a state of joyful doing, when we are forced to do something we do not want to do we are in a state of resentment, and when we are okay with something, we are in a state of acceptance. In the latter, we may prefer not to do it, but we can see the benefit so we accept it anyway. This is why I said earlier, if we cannot at least reach a state of acceptance we are better off not doing it.

This is not to say that if we resent having to go to work one day we should immediately quit our job. What it does mean is that if we find ourself in a state of resentment it would be helpful to pause and reflect. Can we find a reason to accept it? Typically it does not take long to find reasons. For example, if we would rather not go to work and we feel resentful about it, we can reflect on why we are going in the first place. It may be that we want to earn money to put food on the table, or clothes on our backs, and to support our loved ones. The more we contemplate the purpose in deciding to take the job, the more likely we can reach a place of acceptance.

Ideally, we would go beyond simple acceptance and find a job that we can perform joyously. Until then, however, it is vital to reach a place of acceptance before doing anything. Why? If we cannot accept what we are currently doing we would not be bringing presence into it. Instead, we would be pouring disruptive, low frequency energy into the activity, and it is not hard to guess what kind of results we get from doing that.

Several times when I was going to graduate school and sitting at the computer working on a class assignment, I became frustrated to a point of total resentment for "having" to do what was required by the professors. In each case, when I simply walked away from the activity for a while, I was able to return in a better state of consciousness and accept doing what was required of me. In this state of acceptance suddenly the "difficulties" that I perceived moments earlier seemed to simply disappear and the work flowed more smoothly. At times, all it took was five minutes and the peace returned. Other times it took a twenty-minute walk. Still other times I didn't get back to the work until the next day.

In all cases, however, I found not only the experience itself to be much more enjoyable, but also the finished product to be of much higher quality. Further, what would have taken hours of painstaking perseveration was accomplished much more quickly and effortlessly. Each time I found that the resentment turned into acceptance, and then later, upon completion of the task, the acceptance turned into joy. According to Eckhart Tolle, joy does not come from enjoying the outward experience of what we are doing. Rather, it comes from the *acceptance* of our actions. This acceptance, in turn, allows the joy to flow outward into what we are doing. In this way our actions become infused with the creative energy emanating from within.

Taking it a step further, enthusiasm is conceptualized as combining the joy with a goal. When we add a goal to the joy of doing, says Tolle, we become enthusiastic about the chosen activity. This enthusiasm, then, can empower us to produce results that others might see as almost superhuman. And in a sense, it is superhuman, because it is beyond the ego that most people define as us. The enthusiasm then motivates us to continue with the activities that we can do joyfully.

In his book *The Next of Kin*, Megre suggested that fate offers us opportunities only, opportunities to create our future. I read this idea the day after taking the final in a statistics class, knowing I would have to repeat the course. Although I hadn't felt badly about the notion, I also had not viewed it as an "opportunity." However, it was exactly that! It was an opportunity to stick with the program and overcome the obstacles, to persevere! Or, it was an opportunity to move in another direction and use what I had learned in grad school in the next phase of life. At the time the thought of beginning a career in writing crossed the mind. Those thoughts comforted me, and I was able to move forward to complete the master's in psychology.

The incident in stats class was quite enlightening for me. I gave over 30 hours of full undivided attention in preparing for the exam during the final week of the course, not to mention the countless hours I spent studying the subject leading up to that final week. I asked myself why? I was certain I committed as much or more time than many other students who passed the class, and yet I remained uncomfortable when it came to data analysis. Again I asked myself why?

I had the belief that I could master anything given enough time. Was I wrong? Then I started to wonder, was the opportunity presented before me to allow me to whittle away at the intellectual ego? At that time in life I was attempting to shed as much ego as possible. I have been a male for this entire life and was quite aware of the male ego. Similarly, I had been an athlete and coach most of this life leading up to graduate school and was also very aware of the athlete ego in me. The same could be said about teaching, and parenting. In daily practice, I had plenty of opportunity to recognize and shed ego in relation to all those parts of me. However, I had never even considered the possibility of an intellectual ego.

It is helpful to remember that each part of our personal collective ego can be observed with awareness as it presents itself to us. These different egoic entities are typically referred to as different parts of our personality. It is helpful to remember that we have created them, with the assistance of others, in our personal life experience. When we look at the emotion associated with these different personalities without judgment, we are able to digest them once and for all and eliminate the need for the persona in the first place.

Centering all attention on the emotions as they arise is the way to digest them. In other words, by gazing upon the emotion with awareness when it is present we burn up the energy associated with it. This is why I like to use the term "digest" to describe burning up the emotion. It seems to work like the body's metabolism and how it burns the energy provided from the food in order to do work. Once digested, the energy from the emotions can be eliminated from the body in a similar way excrements are released once we have extracted all the useful energy from the food. In contrast, if we attempt to will it away with thought, or turn away from it with distraction (as in directing one's attention to worldly distractions such as movies, food, drugs, sex, etc.) we do not burn up the emotional energy created, we suppress it. This stored energy can, in time, burn us up from within.

Awareness is more powerful than we give credit. And it seems to lose its power in the presence of thought. In fact, becoming lost in thought is what increases the disturbing emotions within. Rumination is the term most often applied to this concept in the psychology literature. However, through direct intentional thought we can create expansive energy, as is the case with thoughts of love and compassion. Thought then, whether it is productive or destructive, acts as a medium to channel the energy coursing through the body.

Once, around three years ago I found myself in a depressed state, brought on by a conversation with B. The feeling seemed to want to draw me in. I realized at the time that all I had to do was turn attention to the life in the backyard and I would feel better. However, I chose not to. Part of me simply wanted to face the ego within so I could let it go. It felt like a humbling experience. I thought at the time that perhaps it takes humbling experiences to release parts of the ego.

So, that day I felt the state of depression and chose to stay in it, knowing that I was digesting emotions. I didn't know where they came from or why they were there but that mattered not. The only thing that mattered was there was something in me that needed processing and so I chose to face it. I felt depressed and accepted it. It felt okay to be depressed even though it seemed to be about something very superficial. Indeed, because it was so superficial it added importance to the need to face and release it. So I did, and as a result, I felt much better in a short period of time.

It is entirely possible that what I was feeling depressed about was not the superficial thought at all. The reason I know it was superficial is I don't even recall what it was, but I do remember at the time considering it to be that. It is much more likely that the surface thought actually stimulated something deeper, something that still needed processed from a previous occurrence. It is important to remember, therefore, that it matters not whether we can trace the feeling to the actual thought that created it. The only thing that matters is we stay with the feeling long enough to digest it. In turn, it will be eliminated from the body forever. And we will feel lighter and more expansive as a result.

CHAPTER 8

Finding Your Center

When attention is on our center we are, in the moment of now, present and connected to the life force that flows through everything. It becomes obvious we are connected energetically when we think about how energy comes into the earth from the sun. It is stored in the plants during photosynthesis. Then, it is passed on to other organisms, including us, through digestion and cellular respiration.

Energy from the sun is not only in the plant. It is everywhere, including the desert, irrespective of whether there are plants to absorb it. The life force in us *is* that energy. This is the place we must learn to center awareness because it *is* our center. It is awareness itself. Our center, conscious awareness, and life energy are all the same thing! Therefore, when attention is moved to our center and that becomes our default setting, or our baseline, then we remain connected to universal source energy. I realize it is a leap to make this statement and I am not asking you to believe it with your intellectual mind, only to experience it for yourself and draw your own conclusions.

Being absolutely present in the here and now is to be free of destructive emotions. On sunny days, all of life seems to stop and rejoice. Stop with it. By remaining in the present and keeping awareness centered on the life presence within, we can experience bliss. What is bliss? It is feeling the expansiveness of life. Life is growth. Life is expansion. For example, if we look at the trees in any yard, where the branches come together they cease to grow. However, once trees are removed, those remaining have branches that expand toward space and continue to grow once again. This is a phenomenon we can see in nature all the time.

It is the life energy in the plants that causes them to grow. And the same life energy is in us. When we center attention on this life force, we feel lighter because attention goes toward open spaciousness that connects *all* things, rather than to the things themselves. In contrast, when we focus on material aspects of the world, the body contracts, and we feel heavy. Which do you think feels better?

What I am suggesting here is that we are intimately connected to the life energy provided by Mother Earth. That is intuitively obvious. After all, we eat food daily, digest it, convert it back to energy, and use that energy for everyday activities. In addition, every molecule in each human body is from the planet earth. It is not difficult to grasp this concept. Further, it is not difficult to grasp the concept that all energy on earth is provided by the sun. However, what is not so easy to grasp is that it goes deeper than that.

The energy provided by the sun is the same energy that is provided by all the stars in the universe, which in turn, provides energy to all of the planets in their perspective solar systems. In its purest sense, all the energy in the universe is the same. Therefore, we are connected to the entire universe. That is how profoundly we are all one body, mind, and spirit (life energy).

71

It is the ego that separates us from this universal source energy. That is neither good nor bad. It just is. Furthermore, it appears it must be so to allow us to participate in life on this planet, at least to some extent. According to some spiritual teachers, if we didn't have at least a trace of ego, conscious energy would leave the body and return to source energy within 21 earth days. When we become the witness of the psychological self we bypass the ego and tap into source energy. This is how we find our center. When we practice it rather than just talk about it, the truth in this idea becomes intuitively obvious.

According to Jung, intuition and sensation are perception, whereas feeling is a means of attaching a value to something. He further suggests that sensation is just as antagonistic to intuition as thinking is to feeling and that one cannot attend to both simultaneously. In other words, the body might be telling us one thing while intuition tells us another. Certainly this has been the experience I have had with regards to thinking and feeling (emotions). If I try to attend to both at the same time confusion sets in and the thinking becomes contaminated by the emotion.

I want to point out, however, that when Jung is referring to sensation, he seems to be referring to outward physical sensations, not inner sensations in the way I referred to earlier, which to me are an inseparable part of intuition. I hadn't considered intuition and physical sensations in this way but it seems to make sense. Indeed, if intuition is subconscious content and connections, as posited by

Jung, certainly physical sensation could act to disrupt the connections of this content.

Jung suggested that we are at a disadvantage when we rely on one of the aforementioned aspects of our experience too heavily because we cannot detect the lesser of the two. In other words, if we invest most of our energy into thinking, we will be less sensitive to feeling and vice versa. This idea adds credence to the practice of mindfulness. Indeed, the more I practice attending to feeling, the more sensitive I become to changes in bodily states in relation to emotions. Similarly, the more I attend to touch, the more aware I become of tension in the body, which may have otherwise gone unnoticed.

This line of thinking is why I decided that while practicing present moment awareness I would give more attention to touch. The reasoning behind this change in practice was due to history telling me that the more I attended to touch, the less I got lost in thought, hence, I became more present and grounded in reality, or rather, experiential time rather than psychological time.

Experiential time is in the present moment of now, whereas psychological time is in the mind of past/future thinking. After making attending to touch a priority during practice, I came to believe that for me personally, the road to inner growth was paved with attention to bodily sensations, not only in the form of touch, but also in the form of feelings (i.e., inner sensations and emotions). This is why I mentioned earlier that to me, sensation includes both internal and external bodily sensations.

73

As mentioned earlier, typically the word "feeling" is used interchangeably with touch (or bodily sensations for Jung) and emotions. However, in mindfulness practice, the two words are separated, presumably because emotions come with connotations of "good" and "bad." In contrast, feeling is neither good nor bad, it is just a feeling. With practice, I came to realize these two terms need not be separated. Indeed, they are both forms of bodily sensations. Therefore, I simplified the practice by turning attention to bodily sensations in general, irrespective of whether they were coming from the sense of touch or from the feelings arising within.

The term I like to use to refer to what is described above is full-body presence. It seems to be supported by the fact that most spiritual teachers and practitioners I have read about begin their practice by silently meditating on the breath as a means of quieting the mind. I now realize the breath is merely a portal to the rest of the body sensations. It is the one that is most easily accessible and therefore, the one that is most commonly used. First we attend to the breath, then to other bodily sensations, and finally, we begin to find that place where neither breath nor bodily sensations are noticed. Instead, we rest in the place of silent spaciousness, or the peace that lies beneath.

What this all means is by learning how to center attention on *all* bodily sensations (including both inner and outer sensations), we become more accustomed to feeling bodily contractions, whether they are large or small. In turn, we can feel tension and emotions at their inception, relax the body with intention, and allow the energy to flow freely rather than being trapped. Our baseline awareness then shifts from thought to full-body presence. Importantly, according to Chuang Tzu, "Once you find the center and achieve harmony, heaven and earth take their proper places and all things are fully nourished." In turn, we are fully prepared to accept and process the emotions as they arise in the present moment of now.

Another powerful example of digesting emotions occurred several years ago when I was experiencing car trouble (always a great pointer). I was leaving school and I heard a grinding noise when starting the vehicle. I was a little alarmed given I had just put over $2,200 dollars into it not long before and even the starter had been replaced! However, the thought occurred to me that perhaps I just held the key too long and that caused the noise. Consequently, when I arrived home I decided to turn it off and start it several times to test the theory. Each time the results were the same, a grinding noise occurred.

As I walked into the house I was feeling an emotional arousal. Thoughts started coming in relation to the disturbing emotions. How could this be? After all the money I put into it, this shouldn't be happening. This is what I get for trying to save money! And on and on the mind went, apparently searching for thoughts that matched the feelings. I noticed what the mind was doing and so I intentionally sent other messages such as, it might not be a big deal, perhaps a friend can fix it, worst case scenario, I could always take out a loan to pay for it, and other thoughts like these. I then decided to go on a walk to quiet the mind.

As I was on the walk I turned attention to the natural environment around me. It was dusk but the moon shone bright. The streets were empty and the clouds were broken. As I gazed upon the trees and the mountains in the distance, the thought occurred to me, this is what really matters! I had found the center, and suddenly joy replaced anguish as I put the car trouble in its proper perspective. Later, as I drove to a former girlfriend's house (I will refer to her as C), I made a conscious decision to let go of the car trouble, be present, and enjoy the evening. I recall saying to myself, be here now, a couple of times in an attempt to remain present.

During the first half of the commute this worked quite well and I was at peace. However, I chose to get off the freeway and take a back road, given that it was rush hour and the freeway was typically backed up. First, it took a while to get onto the road, as traffic was quite thick. Second, the road itself was quite twisted and was very slow going because of all the curves. Third, there was a line of cars behind me causing me to feel hurried. Finally, it was dark and difficult to see, adding pressure to an already tense situation.

Although I did remain fairly present in thought, I was feeling the tension in the body. At times when thoughts arose that matched the tension I laughed out loud, realizing what the ego in me was doing. When I finally came out of the turns I missed the exit I was going to take because it was too dark for me to see the road sign. I called C to be certain I was on course after choosing another route. She assured me I was and it looked as though I was in the clear and would be there soon. However, I missed another exit and had trouble finding a place to turn around. In turn, I could feel a powerful emotional arousal in the stomach region.

Then a very interesting thing happened. The words, "It's SO painful!" came to mind. The second time the same words came to mind I laughed out loud! Immediately, the tension vanished, seemingly being transformed into laughter. Once again I found the center and was free of the contractive feeling. In turn, C and I went on to have an enjoyable evening.

On another occasion, when I was talking to B, whom I was no longer dating, I noticed how the body would react whenever she would mention her new boyfriend. For example, at one point she discussed how fortunate she felt to have his support through all her struggles. When she said it, I felt a jolt of energy as if I was jabbed in the mid-section. Fortunately, attention turned automatically to the feeling and I experienced it with no thought. It seems that because of that, the feeling dissipated quickly. In the past I believe I would have immediately turned to thought, the feelings would have been exacerbated, and we may have even gotten in an argument as the mind asked something like, "Why would she want to hurt me that way?"

Interestingly, facing any unprocessed emotions was one of the motivations for seeing B in the first place. Later, after reflecting on the incident, I was pleased with both the direction of attention and the way the body responded. I believed that I had processed and let go of some layers of ego in relation to our history. In addition, I was quite certain the next time B talked about her current relationship the body would be less reactive. Indeed, that is exactly what happened. To me, this was a great example of how to digest unprocessed emotions with intention.

CHAPTER 9

Digesting Small Emotions

I like to conceive of digesting emotions in the way discussed thus far as the "freedom game." The way this game is played is to start with very small emotional disturbances that may occur in any given day. For example, a car might honk the horn at you at a stoplight. Instead of letting the mind take the thought train on the tracks of human suffering, just stop, turn all attention to the feeling, relax the area of the body surrounding the disturbance, and let it flow. Viola! You are now liberated from the disturbance. With practice, it really can be that easy.

It is helpful to be aware that we do not have to sit and meditate for hours a day to become self-actualized or "enlightened." We must only learn to play the freedom game each and every day. Indeed, life offers many opportunities to recognize disturbances so that we can transcend them. How many opportunities such as these are offered while sitting quietly on a pillow? What this means is anyone, anywhere, in any circumstance can become self-actualized. We need only let go of the idea that it is only for monks and nuns who spend their entire lives in service of God.

At times the ego can appear to be "primed" before actually becoming engaged. A sarcastic joke is a good example of an ego primer. It is helpful to notice when the priming occurs in order to direct the attention in the right way. This is one way the ego can be so sneaky, we don't even know when it has been primed for activity.

Once I decided to mow the front lawn and the thought occurred, here you go neighbor D! And I felt glad that I was doing this because the neighbor D would be happy about it (he often made snide comments if I let the grass grow too long). However, then the ego decided to get more involved and ask, "But will *his* ego get involved? Should I avoid mowing the grass to keep from inflating his ego?" (As in, he might feel like *he* was the reason I cut the grass)

Of course, it was the ego in me suggesting that D's ego might become inflated. How sneaky the ego can be. It almost seems as though it has an entity of its own, and in a way it does! Certainly it has its own psychic energy. Indeed, this is one reason it can have such a powerful influence over us. In the example referred to above, even after I was done with the job the mind asked, did I mow for the right reason? Oddly, the ego was asking itself if *it* was getting in the way of the decision-making process!

If it were not ego, there would be no question, only deciding in total awareness. If we can find the way to live in the absence of any ego involvement whatsoever, the quality of living would drastically improve. This is what the phrase enlightenment ultimately means. It means we are totally present in the now because there is no ego getting in the way. Imagine how nice that would be! Interestingly, when we act from this place of pure conscious awareness it is often labeled as "Godliness." However, this term has such a strong religious overtone it can come across as too constricting for many. This too is ego of course, only it is ego disguised as one who is too "down to earth" to be labeled as "Godly."

It is helpful to remember that everyone is not in the same place when it comes to processing emotions. Some people come up against emotions in such a profound way that they cannot separate themselves from the feelings and they can become overwhelmed. For example, once a friend said that at times she sees ego from a distance and thinks, I don't want that! And the next thing she knows her ego is right next to her. She described it as being kind of "scary." It is for this reason we must take it slow in the beginning. We can start watching smaller emotions, the kind that come up from minor life events, such as having to wait in line at the grocery store, or dropping something in the kitchen. That is if these are indeed perceived as small events. Again, everyone is in a different place.

A good personal example of watching smaller emotions occurred one afternoon after returning from class. B had an emotional breakdown and she said she was feeling despair about her prospect of completing graduate school. At one point as I was hugging and consoling her, I observed thoughts coming up such as, this type of event is occurring too often, and, I don't know how much more of this I can take, bringing with it an emotional charge. I turned attention to the feeling itself and cut the thought train short. The feelings dissipated quickly and suddenly I realized that this is grad school and many people find it extremely stressful. Put in that light, B's emotional frailty seemed not only normal, but also quite expected. That thought seemed to provide me with the patience necessary to comfort her.

However, while I was attempting to console her she brought up something else that was bothering her, giving me the opportunity to practice digesting more emotions. B suggested that while we were on the bike ride home from campus that day, because I was choosing to pass cars by going in between them, it was really hard for her to keep up and she found herself cutting off drivers to do so. I felt the energy build inside of me again but just let it be there and turned attention to it. This seemed to help me accept that she was upset about the prospect of completing grad school and it really didn't have anything to do with me. That realization helped me come to grips with the reaction from within.

A little later in the evening we were getting ready to leave for the pub to have a couple pints of beer. Happy hour was almost over and I wanted to get there in time to get better prices. In all, we would have only saved a couple dollars, but for some reason it was weighing heavily on me. I realized how stingy I was being; as it certainly wasn't worth adding stress to what B was already experiencing for a measly couple dollars. To make matters worse, B offered to buy the beer if we were late, however, when it came time to pay she asked me "Would you like me to pay?"

That put me in a rather uncomfortable position and I felt another internal reaction that captured attention. On top of that, we actually made it on time, but were not given happy hour prices by the server, further adding energy to the current internal experience.

Once again I placed attention on the feeling rather than the thoughts and the energy melted away. I was pleased how I noticed all of these feelings without reacting to any of them. Further, at the end of the evening I was able to share the incident with B without getting emotionally involved, thereby allowing the conversation to be a constructive one. Over all, this event provided me with an excellent opportunity to practice digesting emotions, and I came away feeling grateful for the practice.

Not long after the event described above, B came home from school and I sensed she was again in need of some emotional support. In the past, that type of thought had produced a disturbing emotional reaction and caused me to feel the need to get away and get some space. On this day, however, the thought occurred to me that I might just try and give her the emotional support and see how things turned out. One important aspect of this thought, however, was that it came *before* the emotional reaction was able to take a hold of the cognitive processes, thereby leading to thoughts of needing space.

It is helpful to recognize that emotional reactions produce thoughts that have been associated with similar feelings in the past as a means of using our memory to our advantage. In general, this could be a very helpful adaptation, as acting on these thoughts might lead us away from events that could bring on emotional pain and suffering. On the other hand, it most likely would limit our experiences in the future, causing us to miss out on some enjoyable adventures. Moreover, it may also lead us away from helping friends and loved ones, leading to emotional suffering later, brought on by an interaction with those who want to know why we were not available for them.

When this occurs it is entirely possible to convince ourselves that this is the type of interaction we were trying to avoid, thereby reinforcing the thought that we need space. In actuality, however, this interaction was created the moment we decided space was needed because the initial internal reaction produced a thought that we would have been much better off letting go of. This is one of the efficacious aspects of living life mindfully. We become better at separating thoughts, emotions, and actions, and can make decisions that bring harmony for all those concerned.

In the situation described above, recognizing the internal reaction and subsequent thought as independent of one another provided the space necessary to decide on an action that was independent of both. Ironically, I did not need physical space, rather, I needed psychological space, which is to say, I needed to distance myself from any thoughts or emotions I was experiencing in relation to B's need for emotional support. In turn, because I separated myself from those thoughts and feelings, I was able to provide the support she needed.

It is also helpful to remember that discussing peace is not always peaceful. On another night as I sat playing the guitar, I began to share with B thoughts on how much I enjoyed living a balanced life. The trouble was I failed to recognize that she was in the middle of doing work. Had I recognized that, I may have been mindful enough to choose not to bring up the conversation at that time. As it turned out, she was in no mood to hear me talking about finding peace in the middle of a busy schedule in grad school. I'm sure I must have come across as insensitive. Perhaps that is how I came across to her often when I was discussing peace.

It appeared to me that B was having a real negative inner experience. Of course, the ego in me decided to point that out, thinking it might help. Needless to say, it didn't. It wasn't long before I felt emotions beginning to stir and decided to go for a walk to shake the feeling. I walked around the corner and began turning attention to the feeling rather than attempting to think about what had just happened and why it happened. I was glad about that, as I wanted to handle those types of situations in that way, rather than get wrapped up in the drama that the ego was pulling me into.

I hadn't even gotten to the end of the block when this dog came out of nowhere and charged at me, barking and growling vehemently. I jumped back and yelled out, "Hey!" as I stepped back and held ground. It didn't feel like a good idea to back down at the moment.

The owner immediately yelled at the dog and walked over to pull it away from me. He said, "Sorry about that."

I responded, "Oh, that's alright," and I turned and walked away. I did feel good about the fact that I did not turn the sudden fear into anger and make some kind of egoic comment to the dog's owner. Instead, I was able to separate the two. It certainly was not the man's fault. After all, the dog came out of the garage as I walked down the sidewalk.

This event got me to thinking. Did this dog somehow feel the disruptive energy I was just releasing? Seconds before the dog lurched out at me I had just turned attention to the feeling and felt the tension leaving the body. Perhaps the dog actually sensed this disruptive energy and then reacted to it. I recall thinking that I would be interested to go back and talk to the owner to find out if the dog normally acted that way. Judging by the behavior of the owner, I would say it seems likely that the reaction of the dog was out of character.

I continued on the walk and after feeling more of a sense of equanimity, I began to turn attention to thought. Why did the conversation between B and I turn the way it had? It was easy to find fault in B. After all, I was only sharing positive feelings. However, I recognized the direction of this thought and remembered Jesus' famous quote, "First remove the plank from your own eye before attempting to remove the sliver from your friend's." Immediately I changed the thought to, what could I have done differently? Suddenly, all sorts of answers came to mind. I could have recognized B was working and not brought up the topic in that moment. I could have recognized her internal reaction without drawing her attention to it and instead, apologized for interrupting her work. I could have asked her if she would like to go back to work rather than to suggest she do so. I did none of those things.

One helpful aspect about the story described above is that I did recognize the ego in me quickly and chose to go on a walk to let it go. I was also able to practice experiencing the feeling first before attempting to analyze the event. This all took place in a relatively short period of time, and what could have lasted for a day or more was over in 20 minutes.

Another example of digesting emotions occurred when I was preparing to perform in front of a group of people at a coffee shop, similar to the incident mentioned previously. As we were driving to the place I felt some emotions building within. I began to think that I must be nervous. I quickly remembered to mentally re-label it to excited energy. In addition, I turned attention to it and said to myself, "feelings," and the energy began to dissipate. Next, I turned attention to the present moment by looking out the window at the landscape and said silently, "one." I really enjoyed the way the sun was breaking through the clouds and how pronounced plant life appeared. Everything seemed to really jump out and I felt a part of the whole. It never ceases to amaze to me how good it feels to settle into that place.

While we were on stage I felt very relaxed, as if we were playing in the basement. There were no nerves, no emotions, no moments of being lost in thought, just absolute presence. And what a wonderful feeling it was. I came away from the experience extremely grateful for having the opportunity to not only do what I love, but to shed some ego in the process.

I am quite certain that one of the main reasons I was able to relax on stage was because I had already processed the emotions *before* we were actually on stage. Had I ignored the feelings or told myself something that calmed the inner storm without actually digesting the emotions I would have simply stored them for later. Then, when performing on stage, it is likely that I would have experienced a return of the disruptive energy and the ability to play effectively would have been compromised.

When we do not properly digest emotions as they arise we tend to act in ways we don't always want. For example, a friend of mine, who I will refer to as E, shared a story in which he was sitting in a restaurant waiting to be seated. There was an elderly couple sitting next to him and he watched as a younger group of three rushed to an open seat in an apparent attempt to beat the couple, and anyone else who may want it, to the spot.

Next, E watched as a man next to him, who seemed very much in his own world looking like a predator in waiting, shifted his eyes back and forth to scan the room in search of a seat of his own. When the opportunity presented itself, he pounced! Finally, another man walked in and walked right past the elderly couple waiting patiently for their turn, and took the next available seat, which had just opened up. E described how he seethed as he watched these people and he finally erupted on the final man by hollering, "Really? You're really going to take that seat? You really feel good about that decision?" The man relinquished his seat to the couple who was waiting and order was restored.

E expressed how he felt a little guilty about the way he acted and he went up to the man he had yelled at to apologize and explain what had happened. I expressed to E that he probably expressed himself in a way that was necessary for all those involved. Indeed, it may be that because E made a scene in the way that he did, many more people learned a valuable lesson along with the one who received E's rebuke. However, I would not recommend handling a situation in that way. And neither would E.

Another story E shared was an interaction he had with a fan while performing the duty of a scorekeeper at a basketball game. He was getting distracted by the game and making mistakes when the man made the comment for E to "focus on what he is doing." E apologized several times before the man finally settled down.

After the game E apologized again, at which point the man ridiculed him by writing the names of the players on his hand and saying something like, "Here's the names of the players so you can wear your skirt and cheer for both teams."

To this E responded, "Now Sir, I already apologized. Don't you think you are crossing the line?" The man responded that yes, he did indeed cross the line and the altercation came to an end.

After practicing digesting emotions what we find is that we begin to notice what I like to refer to as "pre-emotions," that is to say, we sense that an emotion is about to arise *before* it actually does. It is like there is a slight charge or type of "spark" of some sort. As we become more sensitive to feelings we automatically turn attention to the feel space and typically, the spark goes out before having the opportunity to ignite a full-blown fire.

Once, for example, I found a note on the desk during the last period of the day at school. The note said simply, "This class is so boring." However, it did not generate an emotional reaction like it might have in the past. It may have been partly due to the fact that I was pretty sure I knew who wrote it, and it wouldn't be hard to imagine this particular young man saying that about any class. On the other hand, I have now experienced pre-emotions many times and have come to realize that it comes from habits of the mind. Moreover, because of consistent practice at digesting emotions, attention instinctively goes to feel space. In turn, if a spark was created from any given event it is put out immediately.

The mind expects history to repeat itself. If we are in a life situation similar to one we have experienced before, the mind expects the body to respond the same. Indeed, that is actually helpful because it allows us to improve our skill when it comes to bodily performances. However, when it comes to experiencing emotions, it only leads to erroneous thinking. Therefore, it is important to pause when experiencing such emotional arousal, feel it fully, and then let it go. Once the emotion is properly digested we can then turn attention to thought and attempt to make meaning of the situation.

Interestingly, the same day I found the note I was offered an opportunity to see how digesting emotions in the way described above can help to avoid conflict in life. A and I were going to stop at the store on our way home from school. However, I forgot the grocery list at home. At first, I felt bitter for having to go all the way home to get the list, which in reality was only a mile away. However, I quickly remembered to change the direction of attention and look for the good that could come of it, as discussed previously. Immediately I realized I could pick up the computer while we were there and use the Internet at the store to check email (I didn't have Internet at home at the time).

I wasn't in the mood to shop so I gave A some money and stayed behind to check email. When she returned she only gave me three dollars change. This was much less change than I had anticipated and it elicited a slight emotional charge. After looking over the bill and noticing that she had spent $7 on gourmet cheese, the emotional charge grew and I felt compelled to say something. However, I noticed the aroused state and instead just felt it and let it go.

A few minutes later the opportunity presented itself and I told A that I would have vetoed the cheese idea because it was more than I wanted to spend. However, when I said it I was not in an emotionally charged state so it was a comfortable exchange. I came away from the incident feeling pleased, as spending money had always been a bit of a trigger for me. Furthermore, I felt grateful to A for all her help with the shopping and cooking. Which would feel better, to be annoyed and angry with a loved one, or to appreciate her?

CHAPTER 10

Digesting Powerful Emotions

Once we become accustomed to watching the smaller emotions, such as those described in the previous chapter, we can begin to digest larger ones, such as those arising from financial difficulties, or an illness in the family. One might even consider labeling the emotions according to the intensity. For example, a 1 might be quite mild, perhaps from being slightly annoyed, whereas a level 5 might be extremely powerful or raging, and a level 3 could be somewhere in between. However, although this is one step removed from labeling the emotions as "raging," or "angry," or "mildly upset," it is labeling them nonetheless and even this practice must be dropped eventually.

When we are practicing the art of digesting emotions we may end up finding ourselves in what I like to refer to as "consciousness purgatory." This term came to mind after reading a quote by Paramahansa Yogananda who said, "In the second birth [spiritual awakening] the body remains the same; but the soul's consciousness, instead of being tied to the material plane, is free to roam in the boundless, eternally joyous empire of Spirit." After reading the quote it was as if a sudden light went on and I thought, I am in consciousness purgatory. However, once we pass through this stage we can enter the state of infinite joy.

So, what does consciousness purgatory mean? It seems that I was in a perpetual state between infinite joy (heaven) and total anguish (hell). Consciousness purgatory, then, is the state of being in the absence of either joy or sorrow. Indeed, it had become the new baseline state with little movement in either direction. Not only had I been non-reactive to those events which would have typically been labeled as "negative," such as when I found the note that read, "This class is so boring," but I had also become non-reactive to events that would have typically been viewed as "positive," such as when I typed the last paragraph to the 200 page thesis.

Perhaps this is a necessary step in the evolution of consciousness in each individual. It may be that, although one must pass through this stage of purgatory, the length of time required to stay there varies greatly. The sooner one comes to accept the intimate connectedness of all things, the more quickly one can pass through it.

Yogananda went on to write, "He will realize that the composition of his body and the universe is not soul-imprisoning matter, but expansive, indestructible energy and consciousness." This quote resonated greatly with me as I had a tendency to see the body/mind as an "imprisonment" that we must free ourselves from in order to live from the place of the authentic self. Rather than viewing the body world as a prison, it can be viewed as a playground. We need only remember a simple phrase preceding action, for the highest good of all.

Remembering this guide and acting from this place is likely to bring forth right action. When taken with the understanding of the intimate connectedness between all things, this position helps inspire us to perform action for the highest good. Indeed, Krishna states,

93

"For, seeing the Lord abiding everywhere as the same, he cannot hurt himself by himself and hence treads the highest course."

One of the most powerful experiences I have ever had in digesting emotions occurred a few years ago after being reunited with a former girlfriend following twenty years of separation, who I will refer to as F. When we were originally together I felt I was very much in love with F and was extremely upset that the relationship had ended. Now here we were, twenty years later, provided with another opportunity to be together again. I thought it must be fate.

We dated for a couple weeks and became serious about the relationship very quickly. She professed her undying love for me and even told her son that I was "the one." The more she talked about us sharing our lives together the more I believed she too was "the one" for me. However, at one point I expressed disappointment that she had not invited me to go with her and some friends to spend the weekend camping on the river. Everything seemed to change from that moment on.

Suddenly, F began to express feelings of being rushed and us going too fast, which was shocking to me given that I felt as though I was following her lead. We had a long conversation about it one afternoon that got a little emotional. At least that is how I thought of it, a little emotional. However, F felt like it was a traumatic event. She compared it to the scene on Avengers when the Hulk grabbed the villain by the feet like a rag doll and slammed him to the concrete repeatedly. According to F, she felt as though *I* did that to her emotions. I was astounded that we could see the same conversation so differently.

The night after the conversation I was feeling anxious waiting for her to call. I kept hearing her last words of "I will talk to you tomorrow" only she never did call. I began to get the feeling that I could not take what she said at face value and it was causing some kind of sick feelings in the stomach. It seemed to me that this feeling was coming from uncertainty. Indeed, after our conversation that day I was not sure how to act. When I was with her she came from one place and when we were apart she seemed to think differently. Because of this discrepancy I was not sure what to do. However, she did seem to want time and space so I attempted to give that to her.

Rather than try to figure out the meaning of the feelings, I simply turned all attention to them. The feelings moved from the stomach to the upper abdomen, just below the chest. I wanted to continue to feel the feelings without attempting to analyze them, hoping that in this way, I would be able to access intuition by side-stepping ego.

Unfortunately, however, I felt like I was playing some sort of guessing game. Did I call her to say hello and make sure she was doing okay? Or, do I wait for her to call and hope that she appreciates the space? In previous life history, I have found that women did not typically want space like men. They generally wanted their friends and family to move toward them and comfort them in difficult times. However, by what F had said the last time we talked, that was not what she wanted or needed from me at that time.

After reflecting on whether or not to text I decided it couldn't hurt to say I hope she was doing well and I hope she had a great day, along with a smiley face. I didn't see how I could go wrong by just sending words of encouragement. At that point I decided I would stick to what I told myself before, that I would not try and ask questions via text; rather, I would only send words of encouragement. Moreover, I intended to come only from a place of love, which was quite challenging at the time given that I was experiencing a great deal of ego in the form of fear and doubt.

Not long after sending the text I received a series of text messages from F that explained what I already knew. She said that she doesn't feel good about the idea of her and I because there was too much pressure placed on her too soon. Interestingly, when we were talking previously F had mentioned that she has a tendency to run away from people in her life. After receiving the series of text messages, and going against what I had previously committed to, I sent a message that questioned why she was now running from me. Immediately she sent me a succession of derogatory, hateful messages that seemed to come out of nowhere. At that point I realized that I was no longer talking to the authentic self that I fell in love with. Instead, I was talking to the psychological self that had been built over a lifetime of relationships with other men.

A few nights later I had a dream that seemed to provide understanding of what happened between F and I. In the dream, I found myself at a high school that I had previously worked at with a buddy I graduated with, who I will call G. G and I got separated and

I couldn't find the way out. I seemed to be going in circles and kept hitting dead ends. I ran across some high school boys that tried to help direct me, but when I followed their advice the results were the same. I recall talking to G on the phone and he said he was with a couple of women who wanted to hang out with us. I also remember trying to get some help from some high school girls who acted callously toward me.

The dream seemed to go on forever before I finally woke up, still lost. While awake I reflected briefly on the dream before going back to sleep. As I was falling asleep I sensed that I would return to the lost place I was dreaming about. That thought was not appealing to me. I felt exhausted and did not wish to return there. Consequently, I chose to envision open space and remembered that in dreams I can typically choose to fly, which meant if I did get lost I could just fly right out. This thought brought comfort and I drifted off to sleep very quickly. Then I slept restfully for the next two hours before the alarm went off, which seemed to happen instantaneously.

When I woke up the second time I looked for the possible symbolic meaning in the dream. Interestingly, the symbolism of the dream of being lost and finding dead ends seemed to parallel how I had been searching the mind for the meaning of why the relationship with F ended the way it had. The girls in the dream, who acted callous and unhelpful, seemed to be a symbolic representation of how I perceived F at that time. The boys in the story, who tried to assist me but did not actually help, seemed to represent the psychological self, who, like F, could not help me to find the way.

Another piece to the puzzle was added when I recalled the nature of a song F sang to me on the last afternoon we were together. The song, *Ain't No Mountain High Enough,* is about overcoming obstacles and F explained, after singing it, how she wanted me to overcome our "mountains" to get to her. To me, this was a symbolic representation of our differences in beliefs (specifically that God is a separate entity than us) and what she wanted was for me to adjust mine to reach her. Obviously, I could not do that. Moreover, I didn't feel it was necessary. I believed at the time, and still believe it, that our ideas of reality need not match our loved ones. Instead, we can simply accept that they are different and learn from one another. Indeed, what is learning if not to be open to different viewpoints that may challenge our own?

The next piece of the puzzle came from remembering a key aspect of the final conversation we had. F pointed toward two questions that I had asked her. The first question was whether she thought it would be a good idea for me to free up Wednesdays so her and I could be together that day. The second was if she wanted me to stay the night, although I still wonder if that is actually the way it all came about. In fact, the way I remember the event it was *she* who asked me if I wanted to stay the night.

F took these questions to mean that I didn't hear her when she said she would like some space. However, I did hear her, and these questions (or question) were to add clarity to what was said and to get a feel for the new boundaries she was setting. Indeed, I felt we reached that understanding by the end of the conversation as F had thanked me for "hearing" her.

The final piece to the puzzle was what happened *after* the dream, nothing. Just before I fell to sleep after the dream I felt uncomfortable with going back and getting lost in the building (or symbolically, the mind) once again. Then, when I pictured open spaciousness just before drifting off I found peace. To me, this represents the idea that peace can only be found outside of the confines of the mind. Further, F could not help me to find it and neither could the self (ego). Only by letting go of the contents of the mind (i.e., the thinking part of "self") and transcending the ego can we find peace, which in actuality, need not be found as it is present always. Therefore, by letting go of the darkness of the ego, the light of the authentic self is allowed to shine through.

Interestingly, F seemed to be pointing to the inability I had in finding her, while I was pointing toward the inability in her to let go of the boundaries that separated us. In essence, we were pointing toward the same thing. These "mountains" were apparently too difficult for us to traverse and the relationship ended because of it. It was not one or the other. It was both of us.

I decided that I would wait eight days before contacting F so that I could give her the time and space she was asking for. The reason I chose eight days was, to me, it holds the symbolism of infinity and I use the number in daily practice, both in meditation and in yoga. Anyway, I decided to just give it eight days and try to completely let go of the outcome.

One morning while I was meditating I felt a pressure in the chest from an emotional reaction, apparently coming from the heart chakra. I kept attention there whenever it returned, which was often, and just felt it. Not long after I finished meditating that morning it occurred to me that the feeling may have come during the same hour I received the last text from F eight days prior, which was confirmed after checking the old text messages on the phone.

Amazingly, when I did send F a text asking how she was doing she texted back, saying, "Who is this?" Here was the woman who only two weeks prior had professed her love for me and said she wanted to be in an exclusive relationship with me, and now she didn't even recognize the phone number that belonged to me! That last text added finality to the relationship. Indeed, that was the last I heard from her.

I once read a poem that seems to help when considering life experiences like the one described above. It was written by Ella Wheeler-Wilcox and the first four lines read:

Tis easy to be pleasant,
When life flows along like a song;
But the man worthwhile is the one who will smile
When everything else goes dead wrong.

I try to live life by the words written above. At times, when things go wrong and I feel pressure begin to rise, it just causes me to laugh, as referred to previously. In essence, I am "smiling" when things go "dead wrong." Every time this has happened I have *always* felt much better. Moreover, the moment I laugh at the ego in me, the circumstances in life have *always* changed for the better. To me, this gives credence to the idea that our external environment will match our internal experience.

Another powerful example of digesting emotions occurred after it appeared a dog might maul me. I was on a walk in the neighborhood and was practicing being present. For the first part of the walk I was very present and attention went toward the scenery. However, the joyous feeling I was experiencing while gazing upon the beauty of nature soon led to me thinking about how much I like spending time with good friends, and consequently, I became immersed in thought.

Not long after the thought crossed the mind I turned a corner and glanced to the left. I noticed a dog that looked like a Rottweiler in an aggressive posture, like it was poised and ready to charge. Even more chilling, the moment I noticed the dog's posture it took off and sprinted straight at me at full speed. I had only enough time to turn and face the dog and for some reason simply became very still. I then presented the back of the hand to the dog, which had come to a screeching halt right in front of me, baring its teeth and growling. The dog calmed so I just waited for the owner (who was in his yard observing the event unfold, appearing dumbfounded) to come get it. The owner chastised the dog as he walked it by the collar back to the yard. Upon reflection, considering the posture of

101

the dog and the look on its face, I was surprised the body allowed me to stay, rather than turn and run.

After the owner had collared the dog and walked it away I returned to the walk. After traveling a hundred feet or so a rush of energy flooded the body. I recall feeling it fully as it was happening. It started in the back but upon noticing and releasing tension by allowing it and relaxing, it moved. The feeling seemed to morph into sensations of energy moving around so I followed it with attentive awareness. After moving to the mid-section it seemed to go to the chest, then down the body and into the legs, and finally, the feet, where it then just left the body altogether.

Interestingly, after the energy made its way through the body I felt a tremendous peace that came over me. Considering the recent encounter with the dog that was quite surprising. However, upon reflection I realized it was absolute presence in the absence of thought that allowed me to act independent of the emotions and free myself from the grip of the ego. At first, staying present seemed to keep the emotions from arising in the first place, allowing me to remain calm in the presence of danger. Then, presence helped me to digest the emotions that flooded the body once the perceived danger had passed.

Upon reflection, when I thought about the dog and recalled what happened, everything just seemed to stop, as if time stood still for a moment. The stillness was broken by the voice of the owner calling after the dog. I could sense the anguish and fear in his voice as he screamed at the dog trying to get it to stop. However, the voice seemed to come through a tunnel. In addition, although I was looking directly at the dog and the owner was a good 30 feet away and to the left of me, I can still somehow remember the fearful look on his face as the scene unfolded, which seems impossible. To me this suggests the absolute present moment alertness that I was experiencing, as I seemed to have a panoramic view of the surroundings. The only word that came to mind that describes the episode was surreal.

Interestingly, I was lost in thought yet the dog took on a posture with me anyway, even though I paid it no notice. Or, perhaps that is why it charged. Perhaps it was being protective with its stance and when that failed to get attention it decided its next step would have to be to charge. And perhaps once it got close to me and I became very present and offered it the back of the hand it realized I was no threat. I wondered afterwards what might have happened had I come from the place of fear and acted from there. For example, if I turned and ran would the dog have chased and attacked me? Or, if I became aggressive in response to its aggression would it have then seen me as a threat and proceeded to attack? I am grateful to be able to ask the questions. To me, this was yet another powerful example as to why I want to come from a place of love rather than fear.

CHAPTER 11

Owning Your Emotions

The following poem seems to capture the essence of this section. Every interaction holds the potential of showing us what we need to learn about our self. All we need do is see each event as an opportunity rather than a threat. The poem is called *The Guest House* and was written by Rumi:

> This being human is a guesthouse.
> Every morning a new arrival.
>
> A joy, a depression, a meanness,
> some momentary awareness comes
> as an unexpected visitor.
>
> Welcome and entertain them all!
> Even if they're a crowd of sorrows,
> who violently sweep your house
> empty of its furniture,
> still, treat each guest honorably.
> He may be clearing you out
> for some new delight.
>
> The dark thought, the shame, the malice,
> meet them at the door laughing and invite them in.
>
> Be grateful for whoever comes,
> because each has been sent
> as a guide from beyond.

Indeed, when we are able to view life's events as opportunities, and invite them into our lives rather than attempt to resist them, they become gifts from the Universe that help us to clear out "furniture," or emotional baggage. Eventually, our house (self) will be cleared and the "unexpected visitor" (disturbing emotion) will no longer be necessary.

There is a story told of the Buddha in which a traveler attempted to derail him by sending him insults in response to his teachings. After three days the traveler could take it no more and he asked, "How is it possible that I have sent all of these insults your way and you only respond lovingly in return?"

To which the Buddha replied, "If someone offers you a gift, and you do not accept that gift, to whom does the gift belong?"

This story points to the idea that our internal state is not dependent on others, no matter what they say or do. However, our *reactions* are often highly dependent on others. In order for the body to take action it must have fuel, through the ingestion of food. However, in order for the body to react, its fuel is supplied by thought. It does not take thought to act, as in nonconscious actions through habitual conditioning, or present moment activity with a quiet mind, which would be much more useful. On the other hand, it does take thought to react, simply by the very nature of the word "re-act." What does it mean when we re-act? It means we act in a way that we have acted once before. In order for that to happen it takes thought. Therefore, thought creates the spark necessary to ignite the fuel of an emotional episode.

Wayne Dyer wrote, "What other people do is not what bothers you, it's your reaction to it." He went on to suggest instead of asking ourselves, "Why do they do that?" we ask ourselves, "Why do I let their behavior bother me?" I have been practicing something to this effect for several years now with great success. No longer does other people's behavior bother me. The reason is simple. I no longer place the explanation for feelings I have on *their* behavior. Instead, I feel the feelings fully before even thinking about them. Then later, after the emotional episode has subsided, I reflect on what it is about the belief system I have adopted that needs dropped in order to maintain a calm presence. However, as mentioned before, this state of alert presence does not happen overnight. It must be cultivated. One simple way to do that is to ask the question suggested by Dr. Dyer every time we find ourselves reacting to the behavior of others.

We can learn to have conversations with people without allowing our egos to get involved. As a person is sharing something with us, we can choose to fully listen without reacting. We can allow the person to finish everything they are saying and pause. During the pause, we can ask ourselves, "Am I hearing this information in the absence of ego and judgment?" If the answer is yes, we can now choose to respond or not. Either way, when we send out return information (even no response is information) to the person who shared, we do so without attaching emotion to it. The emotion, of course, comes from our thoughts, which come from our personal experience relating to what the person was sharing. This is why it is important to maintain a quiet mind while listening.

In the above paragraph I have described what it means to listen mindfully. This too must be cultivated. Typically while listening to others, the mind will be in past/future thinking rather than in a state of alert presence. For example, it may be formulating a response to the speaker while he is still talking. Or, it may be turning to memory about past events that are similar to what he is talking about. Some would say this is relating to the individual and it is part of being a good listener. However, I would suggest that to be a truly good listener, we must hear the person with a quiet mind so that we do not infuse the message with our own story.

If we are projecting the mind into the future in order to formulate a response, we are likely to miss much of what is being said. Furthermore, if we turn to memory searching for similar stories so that we can relate, we are likely to confuse their story with our own. Instead, if we listen with a quiet mind we will hear what the speaker is saying, unencumbered by the mind chatter of the psychological self. Indeed, how many times have you shared a story with another and upon their reply thought that is not what I was saying at all! Or perhaps someone shared a story with you and after you responded, they said something similar to you?

As mentioned above, listening mindfully can be cultivated. In order to do this, I suggest whenever you find that the mind is talking take control of the reigns by repeating, word for word, everything the speaker is saying to you. Eventually you will find that you become so engaged with what is being said that the mind becomes quiet. Then, if you notice it start up again, return to repeating exactly what is being said. With practice, silently replicating the dialog will no longer be necessary, as you will develop the habit of listening with a quiet mind. Then you will *truly* be a good listener.

As a personal example of how our story can get in the way of another's, once B was sharing her thoughts about her pets. I have ideas about pets from past history, most of which were not enjoyable. Therefore, the conversation stimulated memory of thoughts that elicited a strong emotional response. In turn, when I reacted, the thoughts attached those disturbing emotions to the current conversation and the words came out with tone.

When this happens, if we don't recognize the ego was activated, we will most likely believe that we are giving an unbiased opinion. In this case, it would be quite likely for an argument to ensue. And that is exactly what happened with B that day. Shortly into the argument, however, we both recognized the triviality of the topic and chose to let it go. This was able to happen because I recognized the ego was involved mid-argument and stated it to B. In turn, she became aware that the reaction was not due to what she was saying, but rather, due to past experience. This understanding helped her to let it go as well.

Earlier that day I recognized ego appear in a different context. When B was discussing her potential working relationship with a male professor from the university, the ego mind activated. However, I recognized it immediately and let it go. Later when B talked about some people she met in her program and they all turned out to be male, the ego was again activated. Fortunately I had become accustomed to that scenario, however (most of her cohorts were male), and the ego was recognized and released quickly.

Another key facet to releasing emotions that tend to arise around others is how we view the concept of fairness. It must be remembered that the only way this idea will bother us is if we place our "self" in the picture. Otherwise, when we see good fortune bestowed on another we would feel happy for them. This is so because of the mirror neurons in our brains, which allow us to reflect back the feelings we observe in others. It is the reason, as studies have demonstrated, that whether we receive a gift, give a gift, or witness the reception of a gift by another, the body releases endorphins (hormones) and serotonin (neurotransmitters), which play a major part in mood regulation, causing us to feel good. After all, how many times have you found yourself smiling when looking at a smiling baby, or when you walk into a room full of people smiling and laughing?

A great example of the effect of mirror neurons happened to me several years ago in a parking lot at Kohl's. A gentleman approached me and offered me ten dollars to help him jumpstart his car. I agreed and told him there was no need to pay me. The effect that small gesture had on him and others was profound. He was beaming at the generosity, which from a monetary standpoint was actually quite small. In addition, there were two elderly women who walked by and were sporting huge smiles as they watched us. They appeared to be discussing the fact that I was helping this man and turned down the money offered by him.

The event described above is a clear example of the effect of mirror neurons. The gift I gave the man was time and I felt good about it. The man obviously felt good about it as well because he was grinning from ear to ear. Finally, the expression on the women's faces clearly stated that they too felt good about witnessing the gift-giving event.

Mirror neurons are also said to allow us to feel empathy for another. Because of this change in body chemistry (hormones and neurotransmitters being released), we are able to truly feel what another person is feeling. However, it must be remembered that, although we are feeling what the other is feeling, these feelings are still coming from within us. For example, in the gift giving episode referred to above, we were all feeling the same thing, but the feelings were still coming from within each individual. This is so because something in us resonated with the energy radiating from the others, triggering the release of the chemicals mentioned above.

To put it another way, let's assume another person witnessed the event occur and instead of feeling expansive, his body contracted, because he perceived the gesture of turning down the money as idiotic. His initial bodily response was most likely the same as the rest of us. However, as soon as the mind started up and it told him it was a stupid thing to do, the energy emanating from his body would shift from a sensation to an emotion due the mind relating it to something in his past. In turn, his body would contract and it would most likely feel very unpleasant. Obviously, he would not feel "good" about that.

This is not to say that we cannot feel the energy of others. We most certainly do. In the example provided above, the feelings we were experiencing were not emotions. They hadn't reached that level yet. They were still in the inner sensation stage referred to earlier. They do not become emotions until the mind gets involved, such as the example of the hypothetical male witness. In addition, when the two women began discussing what they witnessed, it is possible their feelings turned to emotions as well. However, because they perceived the gift giving gesture as "good" their emotions were in relation to previous events that were perceived in a similar light.

To take it a step further, let's say there was a woman standing next to the hypothetical male. She may then feel the energy emanating from him, and if she were not mindful, she could become confused and erroneously believe the feelings originated from her. Ironically, although the emotions were not hers to begin with, the moment she *believed* they were, they would be. Again, this is due to the mirror neurons, which help us to pick up on other people's feelings. Therefore, mirror neurons can be a double-edged sword, unless of course we are present enough to notice the difference between what we are feeling and feelings coming from another.

Once it goes from inner sensations to thoughts about the feelings, the sensations become emotions, and we are coming from the false, psychological self. What this means is if we remain present we can feel the energy emanating from another and recognize it to be coming from them. In turn, emotions would not be stirred in us. This is the importance of the process described earlier of noticing feelings arise and turning all attention to them, without labeling or attempting to figure out where they came from. In other words, it doesn't matter whether the energy is emanating from another or from us. It is merely energy flowing. It is when we attempt to make meaning of the feelings, or attempt to repress them, that confusion sets in.

We must be diligent in feeling the bodily sensations and accept that they are coming from us. Only then can we digest emotions from past conditioning and release any old baggage that we may have been unknowingly carrying for some time. Importantly, others know we are carrying it, for it is the mirror neurons in them that allow them to sense it. It actually feels heavy. Once we become accustomed to sensing it in ourselves, we are able to feel it sooner and act independent of it. Moreover, when we create separation between the authentic self and the emotions, we can be more sensitive to the energy coming from others and act independent of that as well. Eventually, with practice, we can free ourselves from it completely. In turn, we will feel much lighter and have a greater sense of well-being.

The ability to differentiate between the energy arising from previously unprocessed emotions and energy radiating from others is extremely important because not only can we digest our own emotions, we can also help others to digest theirs. Years ago when A was in elementary school she worked for the school on the safety patrol crew. One day she came to me in tears because the kids in the crew were being taken to an amusement park as a reward and she was not allowed to go, due to the fact that she had quit a few days before the trip.

As I listened to the pain in her voice an interesting thing happened. I started to feel emotional pain myself. I became aware of it immediately and it started to dissipate even as I was unsure if it should. I decided I would just allow it to do what it wanted and that helped to clear the mind. It became evident that I did not want to add to her pain by feeding it with the pain I was experiencing, or by lecturing her about the lesson that must be learned. I knew I had a parental responsibility to speak to her about the life lesson that was made available, however, that was not the time to do it.

Later, as I reviewed the conversation in the mind, I felt a desire to talk to her that night. I reminded myself that now was not the time because the pain she was experiencing was still too fresh. I decided that it was important for me to accept the "wanting" and allow it to be there without acting on it. Next, it occurred to me I might as well turn attention to the aspects of the evening, namely, a beautiful day and barbeque. Immediately, I felt a sudden peacefulness come over me. Subsequently, I was able to enjoy the night and at the same time, allow A time to release the energy associated with the disturbing emotions, which of course, was derived from the attention she was giving to her thoughts of loss.

I would like to add here that it seems I was able to help A in more ways than just giving her time to process her emotions. As stated earlier, when she was sharing her feelings with me I felt emotional pain as well. That pain may have been totally hers and had nothing to do with me. If that was the case, then by turning awareness on it and burning it up, I took on some of the pain for her. However, it is entirely possible the pain was mine. Indeed, I love A very much and to see her hurting causes me to hurt as well.

As I have said several times already, the ego can be quite subtle and very tricky. I may have been placing the self into the story, as in, how could they hurt *my* daughter like that. If that were the case, I would be feeling the pain in me rather than what was coming from her. In turn, by continuing to discuss the incident with her, I might actually direct the pain in me back toward her and increase, rather than decrease her pain. Obviously that is *not* what I wanted to do.

So let's go back for a moment and look at what it means to take the "self" out of the picture. If, for example, we are in a situation where we witness another person do something that goes against our moral code, like pirating a CD, or helping themselves to a soda at the fountain in a restaurant without paying for it, and we feel an agitation grow in us, we have placed our "self" in the picture. We say something to ourselves like, "How dare that person steal like that! I would never do such a thing." Or we might simply judge the behavior as bad or wrong by expecting others to go by the same moral code we ourselves go by.

How could we expect such a thing? Others have not had our experiences. They have not "walked in our shoes" so to speak, and therefore, cannot be expected to have developed the same code of ethics. It is the expectation that others *should* behave as we do that

114

leads us into the experience of disturbing emotions. If we take the self out of the picture and accept that others do not have to behave as we do, we will free ourselves of the burden of having to feel the discomforting emotions that come with the desire to change others. In turn, we will be one step closer to freedom from destructive emotions.

CHAPTER 12

We Can Learn a Lot from a Duck

Eckhart Tolle described how humans are the only animals on the planet who have what is referred to as an ego. In his book *The Power of Now* the author states, "The only animals that may occasionally experience something akin to negativity or show signs of neurotic behavior are those that live in close contact with humans and so link into the human mind and its insanity." He then went on to describe a scene in which two ducks were fighting. After watching the ducks fight briefly he observed them flap their wings vigorously as they fled the area and then settle back into swimming gracefully as if nothing had ever happened.

Tolle related the scene mentioned above to how we act as humans. We tend to hold it inside and build up tension rather than release it like the ducks. Then, when we do release it later after it has had a chance to fester, we release it in unhealthy ways. This is a great example of the importance of allowing the emotion to flow uninterrupted. We can observe the feeling before reacting to it. By observing the feeling, we then gain control of the mind. We start directing it rather than allowing it to direct us.

Once a friend named "H" and I went into a store and when we were about to check out, a store employee began to talk to the checkout clerk about a customer who had just left. She appeared quite agitated and said the customer was, "disgusting!" She said his pants were below his butt and his underwear was hanging out. The clerk chimed in and said he talked on his cell phone the whole time.

Interestingly, the way the clerk reacted after responding to the employee reminded me of the way the ducks responded above. He looked me, raised his eyebrows and opened his eyes real wide, took a deep breath and kind of shook his head and shoulders all over. It seemed that he was attempting to join H and I, who we were joyous and happy, rather than the co-worker, who was in an obvious state of agitation.

While I was observing the event I glanced around the room looking at others. They all seemed to be feeling the disruptive energy in the room. However, H and I remained in a joyous state and as the event unfolded it seemed as though our joy replaced the disruptive energy that was present when we arrived. Upon reflection, the incident reminds me of the idea that the only way to eliminate the darkness is by turning the lights on. On this day, H and I may have provided the light that allowed the clerk to see his internal strife and then "shake it off," *literally*!

By releasing the energy arising we can gain control of the mind. When we become aware of the feeling before the brain does, then much emotional pain can be averted. Typically, we hear information and react immediately to it. We start asking ourselves all sorts of questions about it, such as, how does this sit with me? Immediately we begin to judge it. We want to know if it belongs in our life. This obviously serves a purpose. Somehow, however, we have become accustomed to react with our pain-body, as Tolle puts

117

it, before our authentic self even has a chance to observe it. When this happens, we typically make many mistakes. We begin assuming things and making up scenarios in our heads. Before long, we have completed the entire story in our head, before even getting another person's perspective.

This is why it is imperative to be continually aware of the bodily sensations as they occur and when a powerful emotion, which we previously labeled as "negative" or "bad," arises, we must be alert. We can even conceive of the feeling as the voice of awareness. It is saying, "Be alert! Something important is happening here." We can then simply become very still and present, watch the emotion throughout the episodic event, let it flow and let it go.

It must be remembered that emotional episodes require no action, only observation. This is so because emotional reactions are just that, "re-actions" to past events. In contrast, feelings, or more accurately stated, initial inner sensations, may very well require action. Indeed, that action may have to occur immediately, such as if we are in imminent danger. This is what the fight or flight response is all about. However, emotions are not the fight or flight response. The ducks experienced that when they reared up against one another, and then swam away. Their bodies were in fight mode. Because the fight was merely posturing and no real battle took place, there was stored energy in their bodies, which is why they flapped their wings vigorously a few times before swimming on as if nothing happened. They were releasing that stored energy.

We could take a lesson from the ducks. Indeed, some already do by ~~doing~~ engaging in something physical to release stress such as running, lifting weights, boxing, or a multitude of other activities. In turn, the built up energy from a day of stressful events can be burned off, allowing one to think more clearly. Then, the problems leading to the build-up of stress can be resolved in productive ways.

I remember when I was doing the teaching practicum and working with high school juniors, which meant they were only about five years younger than I was at the time. Consequently, there were several students who persistently challenged the authoritative position I was placed in, making the working environment quite stressful. In addition, because I was new to teaching and didn't have the necessary classroom management skills, it made the situation extremely difficult.

After a particularly stressful day, I chose one of two methods to cope with it. Either I got on the bike and road for an hour, or I sank down on the couch and turned on the television to watch NBA basketball and *Sanford and Son*, the old sitcom with Redd Fox (anyone remember that show?). On the days that I chose to watch TV, I was definitely able to relax and forget about any worries. However, the next day when I went back to school nothing was resolved and the same problems existed. In contrast, on the days when I chose to ride the bike, invariably I came up with a plan of how to problem solve the stressful events so that the next day I had a strategy. I would then follow through with the plan and things would improve.

The coping techniques referred to above have been heavily studied. The first strategy, (watching TV), is referred to as avoidance and the second (creating a plan) as problem solving. Avoidance is typically associated with unsuccessful outcomes, as mentioned previously. In addition, once the coping strategy has been utilized, it is typically related to negative affect (bad feelings), because the problem has not been resolved. In contrast, problem solving is often associated with positive affect (good feelings) and successful outcomes. However, in the example provided above it also came with the benefit of another coping mechanism, emotional release. Riding the bike was parallel to the ducks flapping their wings after the brief altercation. Releasing the energy associated with the emotions helped to clear my mind and allow me to formulate a plan to make things run more smoothly in class.

Taking it a step further, when I chose to watch television as a stress reliever, I was not facing the emotions; rather, I was turning away from them. That is what we do when we use avoidance as a method of coping; we turn away from the stressful thoughts and feelings. That does provide some temporary relief and has its place in stress management. However, after turning away from the thoughts and emotions that relate to the stressful event, eventually we must turn into them to search out ways to improve. Otherwise, the energy will be stored as emotions and released in unhealthy ways, which is why they are often referred to as "destructive." To avoid this, we must learn how to fully surrender to what is, which is the topic of the next chapter.

CHAPTER 13

Surrender Is Not What It Seems

A very important aspect about what it means to surrender is to open ourselves up to what is in front of us. We must take in the experience fully and attentively observe it. Amazing beauty can easily go unnoticed. We must not judge the event going into it, nor force a response because it makes us look a certain way. This same application can be used whether looking at a painting or a person.

The word "surrender" often comes with connotations of quitting. Therefore, when it comes to personal growth, surrender is an important aspect that needs the proper understanding. Contrary to popular belief, surrender is not a sign of weakness; it is a sign of strength. It means giving up the results to the power of the Universe. It means giving up our ego and judgment and allowing the Universe to work through us. In this way, we have much more power than if we were to try and "make it happen" using our own abilities. We get the ego out of the way and access source energy.

Anything in life that cannot be changed must be accepted. Anything else will lead to suffering. We cannot argue with what is, it already is and there is no changing that. I know I have said this already but it bears repeating. When we accept what is, every moment becomes the best moment. It has to. It's all there is.

Perhaps the greatest part of surrender and acceptance is the fact that we must accept and forgive ourselves too. There's no other way. When we can accept and forgive all others, and ourselves, the only thing remaining is peace. Anyone can actually reach this place. All it takes is complete acceptance of "what is" and forgiveness of everyone for everything that has already happened. That is what we are truly surrendering to. We are surrendering to the "is"-ness of life. Those who reach this place of complete surrender to the present moment are given the title "enlightened one." However, it is not as esoteric as most of us believe, as you will see in the remainder of this chapter.

A good example of what I am referring to above occurred while I was in grad school. B was driving me home from the thesis proposal meeting and, after passing by a parking spot, became instantly frustrated. She said something like, "I can't do this!" and broke down crying. I asked if she would like me to park the car and she said yes and ran upstairs to the apartment.

Rather than viewing this event as a sign of weakness, as in emotional frailty, it can be viewed as a sign of strength. Indeed, becoming aware of our internal state, even when we do not have the wherewithal to do anything about it, is still a step toward awakening. Furthermore, by recognizing that she was in no state to park the car and allowing me to do it instead, B demonstrated amazing emotional intelligence.

Given that B was in a heightened emotionally aroused state at the time, the emotional intelligence displayed was even more profound. As a matter of fact, I can remember finding myself in similar circumstances and rather than allow another individual to come in and ease the burden, I stubbornly refused assistance and then exacerbated the situation by attempting to act from the place of frustration. Which approach seems more enlightened?

However, it is important to remember the importance of balance. At times, a situation such as the one described above, when we find ourselves in a state of intense frustration, we may want to sit with it for a while and feel it fully. Then, after allowing the emotions to pass, we can act from a place of present moment awareness. In turn, we will have digested whatever emotions arose, which no doubt was in relation to some previous similar occurrence to the one happening in that moment. Other times the emotions might be too powerful and it would be best to walk away from the situation until we are in a better position to act, such as the way B chose in the example provided above.

Certainly we must have the resources to deal with stressful situations or the strain placed on us might be so great that chosen responses actually add more stress than what is already present. In this situation it may be wiser for us to remove ourselves from the scene and regain our composure. No doubt the opportunity to face that particular aspect of the self will reappear in a future happening. However, the hope is that when it does we will be in a more secure state in which staying and facing the powerful emotions that arise will be more manageable. In other words we can "live to fight another day," as the saying goes.

To expand on the ideas posited above, let's consider being placed in a stressful situation during a time when our personal resources are quite low, such as after a sleepless night, or when the blood sugar level is low due to going too long without eating a healthy meal. In situations such as these it would certainly be wiser to avoid an event deemed as "too stressful" to handle given the lack of available resources in the moment. Then, later when the energy returns after rest or a meal, we will have replenished the deleted resources and become capable of handling more pressure. This is how avoidance can be an adaptive coping strategy that, when combined with problem solving later, becomes a powerful tool when dealing with a stressful event. Moreover, this is what is meant by emotional intelligence.

One aspect about processing emotions that is helpful is to avoid making the ego one's enemy. Many years ago I recall recognizing the ego attempting to get a hold of me, so to speak. As soon as I recognized it I said to myself, rather light heartedly, "I see you ego. You almost got me that time!" Being good-natured about it seemed to help me release it more quickly.

In the past I most likely would have beat myself up about it. I would have said something like, "What's wrong with you?" I may have questioned *my* morals, *my* ideals and *my*self. I may have told myself negative things such as, "I must not be a good person," and ruminating on these thoughts would likely lead to the behavior that brought them on in the first place.

Being aware that it is simply the working functions of the mind, however, helps me to remain optimistic. I can then send positive affirmations instead. For example, I can say something like, "See, you are a good person. You recognized ego and didn't act upon it." I would then be able to release the energy associated with the emotions and happily move on. This affirmation would then be likely to lead to more behavior that reaffirms the perceived goodness.

Another time when I was early in the stages of learning to play the guitar, I realized how important it was to be patient with myself learning new music. I noticed a growing frustration that I was not learning the guitar to satiate the appetite to improve. I recognized the frustration to be energy stirred by ego wanting to build itself up and I chose to simply let it go. I just said to myself, "Sorry ego, not this time. I will show you respect, however, as I see you are very cunning and never give up."

Looking at ego as another entity can be an effective tool to keep it from growing. When we do that, however, it is often recognized as a beast and we may not realize that if we feed it, it will grow. Furthermore, turning it into an enemy is another way of feeding it with energy. Therefore, if we simply stop feeding it, it becomes weaker. Soon it rarely flares up at all. And, when it does, it becomes merely a spark for us to quickly notice, smile at and say, "Nice try ego, better luck next time." Then give it a wink and say goodbye. Try it. You may be surprised at the results.

CHAPTER 14

Suppression Is Not Surrender

A good analogy for facing one's emotions is turning into a slide after losing control of a vehicle, rather than attempting to resist it by turning away. Attempting to turn away, of course, only makes matters worse. Similarly, when we try to avoid an emotional reaction we are likely to exacerbate the problem because we are not dealing directly with it. For example, a person might have a disagreement with a friend and then decide to avoid the topic in a later interaction to reduce the risk of repeating the emotional arousal that was previously labeled as "negative," which is the most likely reason for wanting to avoid it in the future. However, in so doing we run the risk of further disagreements with the friend because of a lack of understanding.

Using avoidance as a coping mechanism in this way could also be likened to slowing down when entering a sharp turn as opposed to accelerating. When the vehicle speeds up it actually lowers its center of gravity giving it better traction and maneuverability. Similarly, when we look at the emotional charge without reacting to it we become more grounded and gain access to better maneuverability in the face of emotionally challenging situations. This is why it can be very helpful to turn into the emotion rather than away from it. It allows us to process the feelings and let them go.

For me, a common yet powerful example of what happens when we suppress rather than feel and release emotions occurred a few years ago. Interestingly, the event took place on the same day that I hosted a meditation retreat in which I mediated for five hours in one day. I bring this up merely to add context to the story I am about to share so that the depth of the meaning behind it can be understood. That morning I woke up very present and ready to enjoy the affair with no thought (or at least very little) about missing out on more pressing opportunities, such as working on the thesis (I was in grad school at the time), or finishing the cleanup from a recent tree removal in the yard.

As people started arriving there was still very little thought. A fleeting thought, such as the desire to get started, would cross the mind and quickly disperse as I redirected attention the now. We began meditating at around 10 am and continued until 3:30 pm, with a couple short breaks in between. When it was done I was amazed I had just meditated for over five hours!

During the meditation there were many background noises from people getting up and getting snacks in the kitchen, to snoring by those who had fallen asleep. Although I was accustomed to meditating alone, these noises had very little effect on the internal condition I was experiencing and even provided additional practice in staying present. A few thoughts arose about whether this was really a good idea, given that it cost me money to meditate at home! However, there was no feeling associated with the thoughts and I just observed them rise and fall like watching waves approach the shoreline before returning to the ocean. I felt very accepting of the thoughts when present which seems to be why they failed to elicit any emotional response.

However, B had a much different experience. She shared with me how she became very frustrated with all the noise and remained in that state for several hours. Still, this too, was good practice, as she remained aware of her internal state and was able to discuss it from the place of an observer later. In this way, she could step outside the victim role and into the role of the witness of her own life experience.

When it was time to finish up we spent a little time talking about our experience. I found myself not wanting to talk much. I didn't mind listening to others, yet I had no desire to share. However, there were no feelings one way or the other. In other words, I really wasn't in a state of wanting (as in wanting not to share) or desiring (as in desiring not to share), rather, I felt I was in a state of total equanimity with no wants or desires. Little did I know this was all about to change.

As soon as the last person left I began cleaning up. I spent a little time cleaning the house before deciding to work in the yard and make a trip to the local home and garden shop to drop off some tree clippings and pick up a load of sand and crushed asphalt to shore up the foundation for a pool I was installing. I remained quite present throughout the entire time.

By the time I finished emptying the back of the truck and placing piles near the area that required reinforcement, it was already

7 pm. I decided that was enough work for the day and that it was time to relax, so I got myself a snack and settled in to watch a movie I had started the night before about the life of the XIV Dalai Lama. Although I enjoyed the movie I found myself feeling a little strange.

It was now 9 pm and although it was still light out I contemplated going to bed as I was feeling very tired from the day. That is when the scope of the evening took a drastic turn. A called me and asked me about going to the Harry Potter movie on the following night. This is something we had talked about a long time ago but we had both forgotten it was coming up so soon.

I felt in an agitated state but I attempted to listen as A discussed all the possibilities. After getting off the phone to allow her to get online and order the movie tickets I decided to go for a walk in hopes of relieving some of the tension I was experiencing. However, before I got off the property she called me back full of apologies and said the movie was that night!

That proclamation created more disturbing emotions within and I told her I didn't feel very good just then and wanted to go on a walk. However, there was really no decision to be made. I just needed to come to accept the situation as it was because it was a once in a lifetime event (it was the mid-night showing of the final Harry Potter movie), and A had her heart set on being there. So, I decided to wake myself up by drinking some coffee and make her dream come true, so to speak.

For the next hour, as we prepared for our journey, I felt at peace. In fact, I felt fortunate for having the opportunity to share such a special father-daughter moment such as this. However, that feeling changed when we arrived at the theater and found parking to be difficult to say the least. After spending about 20 minutes driving around trying to find a spot, success finally came, and along with it, a relief from the growing agitation. I was quite surprised to observe myself become so agitated by such a small, insignificant event, especially given that I had meditated for five hours earlier in the day. I chalked it up to being overly tired and we entered the theater.

The movie was very enjoyable and I was present throughout. A few times I became a little concerned about the behavior of a couple sitting in front of us, as they were loud and obnoxious at times. However, the movie adventure turned out to be very enjoyable and I was glad to have had the opportunity to share it with A. The drive home, however, was a different story.

The moment I got in the truck and began the journey home the agitated state returned. I took a wrong turn and the agitation grew. The next thing I knew I was stuck in road construction at 3:15 am in an unfamiliar part of town. It was all I could do to refrain from going on a verbal tirade in response to the current circumstances. I found myself suppressing the emotion. After all, I did have my 13 year-old daughter in the vehicle and I did not want her to witness that! However, I am quite certain that she felt the frustrations I was experiencing.

After spending 15-20 minutes finding the way to the freeway I was finally able to ask for and receive good directions. Again, as soon as success was found the agitated feeling subsided and I was once again in a state of peace. Although I was very agitated during the two episodes described above, I only lashed out verbally at the predicament for a few very brief moments. Each time I remembered my daughter was with me so I intentionally repressed the feelings. Little did I know that this stored energy would surface the next day.

I only slept four hours that night, as it was 4 am by the time I got to bed. The next day I had to drive back to the city to go to a meeting. As I was driving, a motorcycle approached from behind. I, along with four or five other cars, was traveling in the fast lane passing a few cars along the way. The person on the motorcycle whipped through traffic passing me on the right, honking his horn, and gesturing for me to move over. Immediately, I exploded, raising both hands in the air hoping he would see me in his rearview mirror. I simultaneously called him a derogatory name and debated catching up to confront him over the incident. Fortunately, however, I noticed the reaction in me, realized I was completely over-reacting and that I did not want to be in that state. Therefore, I became very still. I even chuckled a little at the ego in me.

After sharing the escapade with B, she suggested the reaction to the guy on the motorcycle might have been a residual effect from the experience the night before. Of course! Why hadn't that thought occurred to me? It appears that in suppressing the emotion the night before, supposedly in an attempt to "protect" my daughter, I stored up energy that needed only the right circumstances to reach fruition and burst forth. Apparently, the driving actions of the motorcycle rider met those requirements.

To me, this is a good example of the psychological danger of using concealment as a means of coping with stress. It may provide temporary relief, as I don't compound the difficulties by lashing out at others during the ordeal (in this case my daughter). However, that relief could be very short lived if I lash out at someone else a short while later over a completely unrelated incident. In fact, reacting later in this way might be all the more damaging as the anger has been displaced and the recipient is sure to feel like a victim of circumstance, which indeed he would be!

It seems the moral of the story is mostly about prevention. For example, being well rested typically helps to coordinate bodily processes and balance the flow of energy from within. Similarly, the same can be said with regards to proper nutrition and getting exercise. However, another lesson is to be learned from this experience. There will be times when our resources are low since we don't always control the timing of events, such as the mid-night showing of a premier movie. It is during these times we need special vigilance when it comes to aspects of stress management we *do* have control over, such as diet and exercise.

There are likely to be experiences in which we are caught off guard and we will want to be prepared to handle such events. For example, we can choose to eat right and exercise regularly so that the body is functioning as efficiently as possible when a challenging event presents itself.

In the story I have described above, the aspect that seemed to really jump out at me was that of non-acceptance. I so desperately wanted circumstances to be different than they were and that desire created a powerful energy within. I wanted the movie to be on a different night. I wanted there to be parking available as soon as I got there. I wanted to get on the freeway and get home as soon as possible.

The simple formula for what I am describing here is this: reality + non-acceptance = suffering. The movie *was* on that night. There *was* no parking spot to be found upon arriving. And there *was* road construction in the neighborhood I was navigating at 3:15 in the morning. All of those events happened and could not be changed in that moment. The only thing that could be changed was the internal reaction to them.

The question now becomes, how do we reach a level of acceptance of all that is? Moreover, in the moment of a highly agitated state, how do we reach a place of acceptance and move away from the desire to change what already is? It is impossible to change what is. The desire to do so creates tension in the body. This tension leads to psychological suffering. Therefore, the theory goes, just accept it. But that is easier said than done. And in the moment of a charged state it can *seem* impossible. It seems that we must be present at all times to avoid *all* psychological suffering. Presumably, to do so is considered enlightenment. In the remainder of this book, I hope to give you a glimpse into the possibility of ending psychological suffering for once and for all.

CHAPTER 15

Be the Conductor of the Thought Train

Imagine thoughts being the cars of a train traveling down a track. Further, imagine the current emotion as the conductor of the thought train. One of the roles of a conductor is to supervise the crew and ensure both their safety and the safety of their passengers. Another role of the conductor is to ensure the crew understands the orders of the content and destination of the cargo on the train. Yet another role of the conductor is to see to it that cars are added or removed at the appropriate stops along the route. If the emotions had the cognitive ability to disseminate information in the way a train conductor does, it would be entirely appropriate to allow them to be the conductor of the train. This does not appear to be the case, however.

Emotions might be better likened to the engine that powers the train. We have a thought stimulated by an event and emotions are stirred. These emotions, in turn, send the thought train down a given track, determined in large part by previous routes taken by the train powered by a similar emotion in a previous life event. If the emotion is allowed to be the conductor, the thought train will continue down the same path, unaware of crucial factors involved in making an informed decision. For example, in the case with jealousy, we are associating the feeling with other previous events in which we felt a similar internal reaction. The emotion itself might be more accurately described as fear, such as fear of losing the affection of a loved one to another. Or, it might be labeled as anger, as in being

134

mad that *my* loved one would "treat me that way!" However, as mentioned previously, anger is just another form of fear.

I have often heard that there are really only two emotions, fear and love. Everything else branches off these two in one form or another, with all of the so-called "negative" emotions stemming from fear and all of the so-called "positive" emotions arising from love. However, as mentioned previously, there really are no positive or negative emotions, as *all* emotions hold the potential for inner growth by showing us what needs addressed in our life.

Rather than view emotions as positive or negative, good or bad, I like to view them as having either high frequency or low frequency energy. I have used this terminology previously and I would like to expound upon it now. Nikola Tesla, who was a highly regarded inventor and electrical engineer once said, "If you want to find the secrets of the universe, think in terms of energy, frequency and vibration." This applies to emotions and emotional intelligence.

Simply stated, high frequency energy contains short wave lengths, rapid vibrations, and high energy, whereas low frequency energy contains long wavelengths, slow vibrations, and low energy. The rapid vibrations in the high frequency love emotions of joy, inspiration, gratitude, etc., cause the body to feel expansive. In contrast, the slow vibrations in the low frequency fear emotions of anger, hate, shame, etc., create feelings of constriction in the body. Everyone knows which of these feel "better," which is why we come to label them as positive and negative emotions.

Irrespective of how the emotion is labeled, the important thing is to use it as a means of waking up and paying attention. We must first recognize the internal reaction is happening and somehow separate it from the event itself, *before* following the thought train down the track. One technique that can be used to create this separation is using attention to center the awareness on the emotion before attending to the thoughts. This way, we can recognize the emotion as the engine of the thought train bearing down the track of mind, then jump on and become the conductor of that train, discerning between pertinent current information and potentially misleading past events.

Becoming the conductor of the thought train can be rather precarious, however. Who, for example, becomes the conductor? Is it the authentic self or the psychological self? To review, the psychological self can be conceptualized as the constructed self, the one who we believe to be based on past behavior. In contrast, the authentic self can be conceptualized as something deeper than merely the one defined by our actions. The authentic self can be viewed as the witness of the behavior, or the one who might choose to behave differently (or not) given a similar situation. It has often been referred to as the "true self" as a way to describe the person beyond the behavior.

To get past the confusion of whether the authentic self or the psychological self is becoming the conductor of the train, we must first recognize the presence of both. As we discriminate between the two selves and the emotion that powers the construction of the psychological self, we can gain a more lucid understanding of both where the thought came from, and what to do with it. In this way, the authentic self becomes the conductor, the psychological self becomes the crew, and the thoughts are merely the cars on the train, waiting to be dispersed at the appropriate destination.

Interestingly, after writing the analogy above, I came across an article by Matthieu Ricard, who discussed the Buddhist perspective of three levels of consciousness, gross, subtle, and very subtle. According to the author, the gross level contains the emotions and the mind/body interactions with the environment. The subtle level includes "the mind stream that carries on tendencies and habitual patterns," while the very subtle level is pure consciousness.

In the paragraphs above, the psychological self belongs to the subtle levels of consciousness because the egoic tendencies derived from past experience are largely subconscious, making them difficult to recognize. The authentic self belongs in the category of very subtle. It is the awareness behind the thoughts and emotions. Indeed, many are not even aware of this particular self. However, the more we notice the underlying awareness behind the thoughts and emotions, the more we can act from the authentic self. Finally, the "gross" level of consciousness relates to the physical self. Indeed, most of the time it is obvious when something is amiss with the body (illness, injury, etc.).

In the article, Ricard discussed dealing with the emotions before, during, or after they arise. The beginners approach is to deal with them after by recognizing their destructive nature and investigating their consequences. After gaining experience we can deal with them during by asking what shape, size, location, and so forth, does the emotion possess? Finally, we can reach a point at which the emotion arrives without the same enslaving power as it once had.

Getting back to the thought train analogy, let's consider gossip. Gossip seems to lock down the authentic self by creating extra mental noise from the psychological self. This might be where all suffering lies. When a given stimuli enters our life, is it bad *before* we go through the mental construction of what we are to make of that stimuli? If, for example, we experience a bug bite as a tickle does that make it good? Or, if we experience that bite as excruciatingly painful, does that make it bad? Obviously, the bite itself has no value of good or bad until we place that value upon it.

So, if we hear gossip that is good news about someone is it then positive? And if we hear gossip that is bad news about someone does that make it negative? Perhaps the word gossip itself can only be used with "bad" news because it comes with a negative connotation. If it is "good" news then it may no longer be considered gossip.

It seems that it is important not to gossip at all, irrespective of whether we perceive the news as good or bad, for the simple fact that to gossip means to spread rumors that are not confirmed as true. On the other hand, it could be most important to avoid spreading bad news, especially if nothing good can be done with that information.

If we were to spread bad news just to get someone's attention, knowing full well that they cannot use this information to help themselves or others, then we are not only doing them a disservice, but also doing the same to ourselves. Indeed, once our train of thought starts going in that direction, regardless of whether we are the sender or the receiver of the information, it can be quite difficult to turn it back on the course of our choosing.

It is important to remember to not only protect our own thought train and the course it is on, but the thought train of others as well. We can do this by only sharing uplifting stories, while letting go of those stories that elicit an unpleasant internal reaction. If we were to choose to share "bad" news, not only would we be forced to be reunited with the unpleasant emotion, but most likely generate memories of past events that are attached to similar emotions. It becomes quite likely, then, that we would encounter more unpleasant emotions each time a new thought of an old event arises.

As we become more accustomed to feeling the emotions not only do they begin to dissipate faster, but we become more sensitive to the sensations themselves, before they have a chance to collide with thoughts and become an emotional charge. For example, after practicing watching emotions arise and intentionally digesting them for a couple of years, I noticed a profound yet subtle change in the level of consciousness. In other words, I noticed the growth of awareness, which I will attempt to explain by using a few specific examples.

I got home from school one day and went to let B's dog out of the kennel. After initially laying down and acting as if he wanted me to pet him, he growled at me as I proceeded to do so. I had petted him many times in this manner previously and had never gotten that reaction from him before. I felt the emotional charge within me as I forcefully (but not angrily) closed the door and made him stay in the kennel longer, rather than let him out as I had originally intended. This might have actually reinforced his behavior but that is another story altogether.

In the past, this type of event may have acted as a trigger to a much more aroused emotional state. In this confrontation, however, I noticed slight changes, including the behavior of forcefully closing the door to the kennel that resulted from the aroused state. Consequently, I attended to the feeling as I walked away from the kennel and watched it dissipate.

In a separate event that occurred the next morning, I experienced another situation that typically would have produced a much more powerful response. B woke up feeling anxious about school and was acting short tempered. I may have personalized this behavior in the past, thereby exacerbating the situation. This time, however, I was aware that this event might produce a reaction in the body and immediately directed attention to the feeling space just before the charge would have normally occurred, as if to say, "Okay ego I'm ready, go ahead and come if you must." Interestingly, I noticed the spark before the charge, similar to what I discussed previously. Because I placed awareness in the center of the body, rather than toward thought, the emotional episode was averted before it had a chance to get off the ground, so to speak.

I find it imperative to point out that I placed awareness in the center of the body (which is what it means to be "centered"), and I did so with *acceptance*. In other words, I accepted that there might be an emotional reaction and I was totally okay with that. Not being okay with an emotional charge is what suppresses it, or intensifies it, depending upon where the attention goes. If the attention goes toward thoughts of don't feel that way, then we suppress it, whereas, if the attention goes toward thoughts of why we are feeling that way, it intensifies it. In the former we are denying it and in the latter, we are justifying it. Accepting it is what allows the energy to flow freely and leave the body. The importance of acceptance cannot be over-stated.

After reflecting on the events described above, I realized the experience of equanimity was due, at least in large part, to regular practice of attending more to the physiological state throughout the day. For example, I had been driving to and from work with no radio for some time and much of attention went to the current physical state. In other words, I would keep some level of awareness on the body and either, I could feel tension or it would be relaxed. When I felt tension, I deliberately relaxed that part of the body. Furthermore, I had been doing the same thing during many other times throughout the day, such as when talking to others, or sitting in the classroom while teaching and observing student behavior, or while doing the dishes, or on a walk, etc. I concluded that it was the practice of attending to the body regularly, along with noting and releasing any tension, that led to the reduction of emotional reactivity demonstrated in the events described above.

CHAPTER 16

Removing Deep-Seated Emotions

It is helpful to remember that at times, we must process energy that was stored many years prior during emotional episodes that are particularly challenging. Let's take jealousy for example. Jealousy can be a powerful and destructive emotion and often times it goes unnoticed by the individual experiencing it. However, everyone else tends to notice it.

Let's say our significant other calls us from out of town and informs us that he or she is planning on going to dinner with an old friend. Typically our society frowns on this type of behavior and some societies even forbid it altogether. The reason is simple. Jealousy can cause people to act in ways they would not normally act. The jealousy we come up against might be our own, coming from personal experience from our past, or it could be imposed by the ideology of our society. In either case, we typically feel a powerful contraction in the abdomen.

Why the abdomen you might ask? The abdomen is the general location of the solar plexus chakra, which has much to do with a sense of control. Briefly, there are 7 major chakras that make up the energy system of the body. The top chakra is the crown, located at the top of the head and represents our ability to connect spiritually with the Universe. Next comes the brow chakra or third eye, located in the middle of the forehead and helps us to access intuition. Next is the throat chakra, obviously located in the throat, and helps with self-expression. Then comes the heart chakra, located in the chest and assists with feelings of love and compassion. Next comes the solar plexus referred to above. Just below that is the sacral chakra, which helps provide a sense of abundance and well-being. Finally, at the base of the spine is located the root chakra, which helps us to feel grounded. Together, the chakras help us to live a balanced and harmonious life, assuming they are healthy and in balance.

In the case of jealousy, one of the major aspects we are experiencing during the emotional episode is the fear of a loss of control, as in, our loved one might leave us for another and there is little we can do about it. It is for this reason that we typically experience strong contractions in the abdomen region. We are resisting the perceived loss of control we are currently experiencing.

Why do we resist it? This question goes back to what I wrote a moment ago that we might have picked up the idea of proper social behavior from society. In this case, if our partner's behavior does not match what we have come to identify as "proper" or "respectful" social behavior, such as having dinner with someone who is the opposite gender, then what we are observing does not match our belief system (or egoic belief). In turn, tension is created in the body and we typically feel this tension in the solar plexus, in the form of a contraction.

And why does the body contract? As mentioned before, fear is low frequency energy and it creates a constricting sensation in the body. Furthermore, the ego is what separates our life energy from the source. Therefore, if we can let go of the ego we can be in line with the universal force of life (e.g., growth, expansion, etc.). However, keeping attention on form will cause the body to contract, leading to suffering. In contrast, keeping attention on the formless leads to freedom through expansion.

Perhaps anyone can relate to the vastly different experiences of contraction and expansion. If attention is on form, the body contracts, as form is contraction by its very nature. Think about it. Something, some force, is pulling molecules and atoms and particles together to manifest form. Without it we could have no experience. Yet in order to experience the oneness in it all, we need only place attention on growth and expansion.

It has been estimated the average person has somewhere in the neighborhood of 50 to 70 thousand thoughts per day. However, when we stop and pay attention, we will see that they are very repetitive. Of course they are! They are coming from the subconscious mind sending messages to the conscious mind based on something the authentic self needs to undergo for personal growth. The authentic self, or life force within us, "wants" (for lack of a better term), to grow. Why would it not? As mentioned previously, all of existence seems to want to experience growth in some way. And, when the life energy is suppressed by ego what happens? We experience contraction in the form of emotions and we suffer. Until, of course, we can witness the emotions with non-attachment.

This is where conceiving of the ego as a system with the ability to make us more alert or to "awaken" comes in. What this means is we become the witness of the energy that is fluctuating throughout the day and continually allow it to flow by fully feeling it and allowing the body to relax. By getting closer and closer to the goal of total presence, we learn about the self. And then we can become independent of it. This is what it means to be "liberated" from the grips of the ego.

The story is similar if we developed the belief system on our own, based on previous life experience. However, the explanation becomes much more complicated, because often times, we don't know where the feelings are coming from. Therefore, it is common to make the assumption, "that's just me; it's the way I am." Let's take a closer look at this assumption and see if it has any merit.

Let's return to the scenario of our significant other informing us of his or her intention to have dinner with a friend of the opposite gender. Perhaps in college we experienced a partner being unfaithful to us and it took us a long time to get over. Actually, if the energy we are experiencing in the now is due to a previous event, we have not gotten over it! Or, perhaps it has to do with our own indiscretions while in a past relationship. Or it may be due to the break-up of our parents when we were young and now we have a fear the same will happen to us in our relationships. Or it might be a combination of any of these factors.

Whatever the case may be, jealousy is not something we want to foster because it *never* helps us get what we truly want, which is love. It might help us to control another individual, but that will not bring us the love we are looking for. At best, it will only bring us compliance, and at worst, it will drive others away from us. It may even cause us to act in a way that we regret for the rest of our life. Therefore, we might consider being grateful when the opportunity arises to expose it, place awareness on it, and let it go.

Even if the thought of our partner being unfaithful appears over and over in the mind, it does not mean that he or she would choose to do so. It only means we have unresolved issues. If when each of these thoughts appears we watch and accept them and look for any emotions that come with them, we will be able to slowly digest them. With continued effort of alert awareness, we can process all of the old baggage we have accumulated from years of relationships.

Typically, what happens in the kind of situation described above is when we first hear of our partner's plans it triggers a strong reaction, that is of course, if we have issues with jealousy (or anger, or anxiety, or any other destructive fear emotion). If, when the thoughts come, we quickly turn attention to the feelings, the energy will begin to dissipate. However, we normally get drawn back into thought and only a small percentage of the energy gets digested. The rest gets fed to the mind for thinking. What is it thinking about? It is thinking about why the body is feeling the way it is feeling. Why is it thinking about that? That is one of the functions of the subconscious mind. It will continue to send us thoughts until we make a plan as to what to do with it. Or, until we become accustomed to watching the thoughts and letting them go.

It is helpful to remember that it is not the thinking that is the problem. It is the becoming attached to the thoughts being presented that poses the problem. And it is identifying entirely with the mind that gets us into trouble. Again, it is wise to remember that a thought is just a thought. It is not asking you to believe it, only notice it.

Going back to the typical jealous reaction, after the initial trigger and subsequent emotional response, as long as we are able to watch the feelings for a moment before getting drawn back into thought, then we are likely to digest part of the emotion in that moment. We might then drift back into thought for a while and stir more emotions, which is to say, more energy from previous life history begins to get released. That energy either gets used by the mind to form new belief structures supported by jealous thoughts, or it gets burned up in the light of awareness as we watch it. The more we watch it, the more that gets burned up, and the more we direct attention to thought, the more the associated energy gets trapped in the body.

If we digest a portion of the stored energy right after being triggered by attending to the feeling instead of thought, and we repeat this practice after the thoughts return, then it is very likely we will burn up more energy by returning to the feelings on the second go around. In addition, if each time the jealous thoughts come up we once again turn attention to the feelings instead of the thoughts, we will continue to digest the emotions until all the energy associated with them is gone. Again, this applies to *all* destructive emotions.

The process described above is analogous to holding a balloon by the stem and slowly releasing the air. We might release all the air during a single session by holding the stem open and watching the air leave the balloon. Or, we might let out a little air, then tie the stem up for a while and walk around with the balloon in our pocket, waiting until the next event comes along that reminds us of the balloon we have safely stowed away. Then, we take the balloon out, untie the stem, and allow more air to dissipate. Or, we may come across some poor unsuspecting soul who pops our balloon and suffers the repercussions of our emotional outburst.

Although the drawn-out method described above does work, it can take a very long time, even many years. This is what happens with avoidance. We might reduce the present moment stress we are experiencing by distracting ourselves with something else. However, we are simply storing the balloon in our pocket until the next time. Better to keep the balloon out and let the air out completely the first time. The way to do this is to keep attention on the feelings until the emotions can be completely digested. Then, if thoughts similar to the triggering thought appear later, they will not carry old stored energy from the past. In this way we will be better able to trust our feelings as they occur in the present moment.

During any typical emotional episode like the one described above what happens is much of the energy gets released during the initial approach. Then, a little more energy is shed with each subsequent emotionally triggering thought. It is possible this train of thought (returning to the thought train analogy) will continue to run through the mind track, looking for compatible cars (similar thoughts) to pick up along the way. Each time the train adds cars to its load, the energy gains more weight. However, if we continue to attend to the energy itself, that energy cannot be used to pick up other cars (thoughts) for the train. In turn, the mind may continue to run, but the train is empty and the cars carry no weight. This means we might actually continue to be faced with thoughts of jealousy. However, they no longer stir any emotion and we are more likely to discount them.

When it comes to digesting emotions, if there is stored energy that needs released, eventually an event will occur that creates a thought that reminds us of the past. Then the body recreates the internal experience associated with that memory. However, if we are not awake, we will mistake the present for the past.

When we practice digesting emotions in the way described throughout this book we begin to realize one common aspect that stands out is the personalizing of the event. The mind will typically create a story that attempts to explain why we are feeling that way. Often times the mind refers back to the other similar situations that occurred previously in our lives, as in, "This is just like that other time when..." What comes next matters not. It is already a lie. There is no way it is *just* like any other time.

When we first begin to practice digesting emotions, we might follow the thoughts for a long time before we remember to turn attention to the feeling. However, in time we will begin to become more aware of this tendency and become better at attending to the feeling without getting lost in thought. All of these thought, feeling, processing, accepting, and releasing events are helpful. They remind us of the wonderful opportunity to rid ourselves of jealousy, or any other destructive emotion we may be experiencing. Before long, attending to the feelings will be the default and we will, in effect, put an end to the thought train before it starts down the track.

It may seem quite challenging to figure out why certain thoughts cross the mind so often, but fortunately, that is not necessary. However, it is helpful to notice whether or not it comes with emotional energy. If the thought comes with emotion, it is telling us we have something to process. If it comes with no emotion, it is telling us that we have been successful at separating ourselves from the emotion, thought, and or event that elicits them. This is a sign of progress.

With practice, the process of digesting emotions will come naturally and we will become more in tune with our feelings. In other words, it will become an automatic response to notice the feeling and turn attention to it rather than the how, what, where, and why the thought was produced. In the jealousy example, we may have seen the thought, known it was jealousy, and suppressed the feelings before they had a chance to get going. But if that was the case we will certainly get another opportunity because we will be carrying the balloon in our pocket. Indeed, if we fail to digest the emotions completely in the first go around, we *will* have the opportunity to break down barriers of the ego, created by the mind in its never ending quest of identity development.

CHAPTER 17
Digesting Emotions & Awareness

The more we pay attention to emotions before thinking about them, the greater awareness becomes. I mentioned a few examples of this earlier. I would now like to elucidate this idea further. For example, as a result of paying more attention to the bodily reactions, I noticed that the difference between pride and peace can be quite subtle yet incredibly profound.

When we feel a sense of pride it can typically be felt in the body and has a kind of weight to it. It seems to occur in the chest area, as in the saying "his chest filled with pride," and feels confining. More specifically, the chest feels swollen yet constricted and in turn, the individual typically stands taller with the shoulders back and the chest slightly forward. Consider the phrases " a prideful walk," and "he stood a little taller that day." In contrast, when we feel peace, there is no feeling experienced in the body and it comes with no "weight" to it. Furthermore, there is no feeling of confinement as there is in the case of pride. Instead, we feel expansive or bigger than ourselves, as if there is no separation between self and other.

If we consider the difference between pride and peace described above, we can see how pride can end up causing suffering, which is why pride often connotes negativity, such as, "she was forced to swallow her pride," and "her pride got the best of her," etc. If, for example, a person is told that she looks good and feels a sense

153

of pride building in the chest area, the energy is likely to get stored in the body and eventually will have to be released. One of the most common ways of releasing the energy stored in the form of an emotion is to meet up with the opposite emotion, in this case shame.

When we encounter so called "positive" emotions (e.g., pride) and attach them to our self-identity (i.e., "I am a good looking person") that energy gets stored. The self-identity that had been built with the prideful incident must be shed in order to release the stored energy. Typically, that creates suffering. Indeed, when we attach our self-worth to something someone says to us, eventually we will come across another who says something else (e.g., "You are ugly!"), triggering the release of that energy, often in the form of anger (e.g., "How dare you say that to me!"). Or, we might simply feel depressed and the chest, once filled with pride, now deflates in the presence of shame. This is what allows the body to return to a state of equanimity.

When we undergo too many life events in one direction or another (too much pride or too much shame), balance is disrupted and the system is not allowed to work at its optimum level. When the give and take of the energy system works in balance, we are faced with the waxing and waning of emotions as they are allowed to shape and re-shape identity on a continual basis. However, if we face the fluctuating emotions *as they occur* in the now, then we can release the energy by simply letting it flow in the present moment. In turn, no self-identity would be attached to the energy and therefore, none would have to be let go of later. Instead, we would live in flow always.

In the example provided above, if we were to recognize the pride as it manifested itself and simply let it go, we could remain in a state of equanimity and avoid the tsunamis of emotional storms. This is not to say that we avoid emotions all together, merely that we can maintain the type of balance necessary to feel deep inner peace on a more consistent basis.

The more we practice digesting emotions, the more we are able to remain in the state of equanimity referred to above. For example, when I first began mindfulness practice, the subtlest aspect for me was attending to feelings, at least while sitting quietly and trying to notice any feelings that might stir. However, after practicing mindfulness meditation for several months I began to be more sensitive to subtle emotions that would arise while sitting. Not long after that I became aware of the emotion as it first arrived, similar to how I described earlier in the form of a "spark." This early awareness allowed me to look at it, accept it, and let it flow through me without hesitation. It felt like reaching another level of mindfulness and I enjoyed the results.

Digesting emotions also helps us to become more aware of the motive behind our actions because the mind is not clouded by those emotions. For example, one night I was talking to B and I mentioned to her that I had skimmed the pool earlier in the day. She responded by saying that every time I said something about the pool she felt a little guilty (due to the fact that she was the inspiration behind me getting the pool in the first place). After she said that, it suddenly occurred to me that a part of me actually *wanted* her to feel guilty because that aspect of the psychological self blamed her for having to maintain the pool. Once I was aware of that part of me, I was able to let go of it. In turn, I no longer brought the subject up.

Another example of increased awareness occurred not long after that. B and I went to a store to pick up a bottle of wine for a party we were headed to. As we stood in an isle and pondered what to get in addition to the wine, I had a very uncomfortable feeling and wanted to leave. Fortunately, B was very understanding and so we did just that. I had no idea why I felt the way I did, and still don't, but the feeling was strong.

An interesting aspect of the event described above was that attention was more drawn toward feeling than thought, which was the opposite of how it used to be. It seems that by practicing turning attention to the emotional charge as it occurred, rather than to the thought that accompanied it, I had shifted the mental habit to one that was healthier for me. Healthier in that I was able to fully feel the energy within and then accept it and let it go. In contrast, if I were to turn attention to thought, the energy would likely be suppressed rather than released. This, of course, opens the possibility of releasing it later in a very destructive way, such as mentioned previously.

Because of this new habit of the mind, I was able to return quickly to a state of equanimity. Moreover, in a short period of time I found myself in a state of joy. This, no doubt, had a positive influence on others around me. As a matter of fact, while at the party I was sitting on the couch feeling joyous, and before long there was a whole group of people sitting around me. I wasn't doing or saying anything out of the ordinary. In fact, I was saying very little. Instead, I was just sitting there feeling wonderful. It was as if others could sense the expansive energy radiating and were drawn to it.

Then, a very interesting thing happened. As soon as I recognized what was occurring, the ego became active. The thought occurred to me that perhaps other guys would get jealous because all the ladies in the place seemed to be flocking around me. Moments later, the group dispersed. It seems that the egoic thought transformed the feeling I was experiencing from the love-based emotion of joy to the ego-based emotion of pride. This slight shift may have then changed the energy radiating from the body to cause others to decide to move away. This decision must have been completely subconscious because again, I wasn't really saying anything.

An even subtler example of the benefits of being more sensitive to emotions as they arise occurred once when on a walk with B. We were walking around a school with her dog and suddenly B's expression changed in relation to our conversation. I don't even remember what we were talking about but both she and I became aware of her emotional arousal immediately, as it was written all over her face.

B made the decision to go walk on her own for a few minutes while I found a place to sit and watch the swifts settle into the chimney for the night. The swifts are a type of bird that returns twice a year to sleep in the chimney of the neighborhood elementary school. Each night for a couple of weeks tens of thousands of these little birds swirl around, forming a giant funnel, and when the time is right they start pouring into the chimney. It is a beautiful thing to behold and draws a large crowd to witness the spectacle.

I was pleased with B's decision as it takes a great deal of mindfulness to notice the aroused state and act independent of it. I was also pleased that it did not create more than a stir in me. I could sense a slight tension in the face and so I recognized, accepted, and released the energy associated with the change all in one motion. Because I did not feed her emotion we were both able to process and release the energy stirred more quickly and enjoy the rest of the evening.

A regular practice that helped me to learn to digest emotions has been to journal about daily experiences. Not long after writing about the events described above, I realized that the consistent journaling I had been doing played a mediating role toward remaining in a state of equanimity. Indeed, I was processing thoughts and keeping attention centered on the mind/body experience throughout the day as a result of reflection through writing.

The practice of centering attention on the body has the salutary effects of seeing the emotions as they rise and fall during the course of the day. Observing the emotions in this way seems to serve two purposes. First, it separates the emotion from the thought,

158

creating a mental space (or gap) and allows us to operate independent of the thoughts and emotions themselves. In turn, we can use the inner sensations to "wake up" in the moment and pay close attention. Once we become more present we are better able to act in the way that serves us best.

When we are digesting emotions, what we are really doing is shining the light of awareness on them, and in so doing, we become more aware of their origin. This concept can be likened to walking into a dark room and turning the light on. The light does not overpower the dark; rather, it transforms it so there is no longer any darkness. Becoming enlightened, then, is a matter of keeping the light on and continuing to shine it on our shadow, because the moment we turn the light off, darkness reappears.

In sum, by paying attention to the emotions as they arise and remaining centered on the mind/body experience throughout the day, we are provided with opportunities of processing the feelings in their infantile stage, before they are allowed to take a hold of the psychological self. In turn, we will continue to look at life events as they really are and in so doing, we can keep the ego from reappearing and hiding the light of awareness from us once again.

CHAPTER 18

Suggestions for Mindfulness Practice

In the above paragraphs I have discussed mindfulness in relation to processing stored emotional energy, referred to as digesting emotions. I also mentioned that it is important for each person to begin where he or she is right now. Although it is entirely possible to follow the suggestions prescribed thus far and reach a higher level of inner freedom, and with it complete liberation from destructive emotions, it is helpful to practice mindfulness in all areas of our life. In the following chapter, I will attempt to briefly provide examples of how to do just that.

First, I would like to outline a very simple mindfulness-training program anyone can do, and then provide a few examples as to how this program can be incorporated into daily life. As mentioned previously, when I was in the first year of graduate school I took a Contemplative Education class in which we were taught mindfulness practice as prescribed by Shinzen Young.

In the class we were instructed to focus on one aspect of sense perception at a time. For example, I have discussed turning attention to inner sensations and labeling them as "feelings." The other two inner sensations to practice focusing on is the inner dialog or mind chatter, which can be labeled as "talk," and any images that come to mind, which can be labeled as "image." In addition, we were instructed to focus on outer sensations of sight, sound, and touch while labeling them as such.

The technique discussed in the paragraph above is called noting and labeling, and it is done as a method of removing any pre-established labels that have been habituated by the mind. At first, I didn't really like the idea because I was attempting to create the habit of the mind of non-labeling. Naturally, the idea of labeling sense perceptions seemed counter-intuitive to that. However, I realized that the words used above come with no connotations of good or bad, positive or negative. For example, when we label the inner dialog as "talk," we are not adding any value to it; rather, we are just noting that the mind is talking. The same can be said for each of the labels used for the other five sense perceptions mentioned above. Moreover, rather than labeling the object of perception, we are labeling the perception itself.

To take it a step further, consider when we see a bird, or a tree, or a car. Typically, the mind will start asking questions like, I wonder what kind of tree that is? Or, it might make a statement such as, that sure is a pretty bird, or I wish I had a car like that. By noting and labeling the perception (i.e. "sight") of the object in our field of view, we are interrupting the mind chatter and creating a gap. I have referred to this gap often thus far. The idea, as mentioned previously, is to increase this gap. With practice, that is what happens naturally. In turn, the mind becomes quieter.

In order to become more sensitive to feelings as they arise, it is helpful to sit for at least 10 minutes (preferably longer) and turn attention to the inner body. In order to do this, first turn all attention to the breath. Feel the breath entirely as it goes into the nose and

161

then let it out through the mouth. Feel the lungs expand as they fill with air. Then feel the lungs deflate as the air leaves the body through the mouth.

Continue attempting to turn all attention to the breath for several minutes, and as doing so, simply allow the body to relax. Let the breath flow naturally without attempting to force or direct it. If mind chatter distracts you, you can count one on each in-breath and two on each out-breath. Continue to count for several minutes until the mind begins to clear and the body begins to relax. Then, whenever you feel an inner sensation, label it as "feeling," and keep attention on it as long as possible.

The key is to continue to observe it nonjudgmentally, without trying to figure out why it is there. I mentioned this earlier several times. If there are no inner sensations, then you can simply say the word "relaxed," to indicate *that* is the state of the body in the moment. And then return to sitting quietly while attending to the inner body. In the beginning, it is helpful to repeat the word relaxed every 8 to 10 seconds if no feelings seem to be appearing. However, with practice this will no longer be necessary. Instead, you can just sit quietly and direct attention toward your center and wait. If nothing comes up, fine, just be still and relax and enjoy the quietude.

Typically, when we first begin to practice mindfulness in this way, there will be a lot of mind dialog that interrupts the solitude. That is okay too. Just let the thoughts pass like clouds moving across the sky. In addition, you can redirect attention to the feeling space and continue the practice as described above. Again, with practice the mind will begin to quiet.

The reason I have begun with feelings to describe this practice is this entire book has been about digesting emotions. Therefore, it seems to make sense to start the discussion from here. However, when practicing mindfulness, I recommend you begin with thoughts, as they seem to be much more conspicuous than feelings. So, similar to what was described above, sit quietly for at least 10 minutes and turn attention to thoughts. When you notice the inner dialog say to yourself "talk" and just observe what happens. Again, it is extremely important to observe these thoughts nonjudgmentally. Do not concern yourself with how much or how little mind dialog there is. Just watch it.

If there are no thoughts you can label it "quiet" and continue to sit in a relaxed state. In fact, if there are no thoughts the body will most likely be relaxed, as it is typically the thoughts that elicit the contraction of the body in the first place. About every 8 to 10 seconds say to yourself quiet and rest there. When you notice the mind dialog start up again, label it as "talk."

Keep in mind that when you first begin practice you may forget to say talk. It is entirely possible that, because the mind tends to talk incessantly, one is not accustomed to noticing when it is talking. Therefore, you may go much longer than 8 to 10 seconds before remembering to say talk. That is okay, just keep observing and labeling as you notice it. The more you practice the easier it will be to notice when the thoughts appear and disappear, along with the gap between them. The more you notice the gap and attend to that, the longer the gaps become. This is what causes the mind to become quieter. You are creating the habit of a quiet mind by focusing on the gap between thoughts. This is the gap that I have referred to often. And it is in that gap where peace can be found.

After practicing in this way, it is helpful to increase the sitting time, perhaps to 15 minutes, then 20 and so forth. Before long you will be able to sit comfortably for a half hour or more. Moreover, you will begin to enjoy this quiet time as it is extremely rejuvenating for the body. In fact, I have found that thirty minutes of meditation is much more refreshing than a two hour nap. I always come away from meditation feeling revitalized. However, rarely did I feel that way after a nap. Now I no longer take naps, but I meditate daily.

The two aspects of sense perception discussed above are both internal. The third inner sensation is that of images portrayed by the mind. You can learn to watch images in the same way as feelings and thoughts, only this time when noticing just label them as "image," and if there is nothing, label it as "blank." If no images spontaneously arise, you can intentionally create your own. Then, you can try zooming in and out of the image. This particular practice can be a great exercise in attention control.

For example, you can picture an orange in the mind's eye and zoom in on it until you can see the dimples on the skin of the orange. Then zoom in even further and imagine you can see inside the orange. Try and image the tough white skin that holds the segments

164

of the orange together. Then, imagine zooming in further to one individual segment and notice the white fibrous material that separates it from the others. Visualize the juice inside the segment. Finally, imagine you can see the seeds of life in the center of the segment of the orange. Similarly, you can zoom out until the orange becomes as small as a ping-pong ball, then a pebble, and then a grain of sand. In turn, you will increase your ability to sustain attention to that which is desired, instead of letting the mind run wild.

In addition to focusing in on the inner sensations of thought, feeling and image, you can practice focusing out on sight, sound, and touch. However, rather than sitting quietly, I have found it to be more effective to practice while partaking in regular life activities, such as driving, eating, and walking. For example, while driving I have found the slogan leave space and maintain pace to be quite useful.

While you are driving, be mindful to leave plenty of space between you and the car in front of you. The faster you are traveling the more space you will want to leave. Then, simply maintain pace with that vehicle. In personal experience, if someone else wants the spot in front of me, they simply pass me and take it. Then, I leave *that* vehicle the same amount of space. Eventually, someone will end up behind you that prefers space as well, and they will leave you the same as you leave the car in front of you. It is not hard to imagine how much stress will be reduced from driving with more space. Moreover, I have found this practice to be effective even in rush hour traffic!

While you are driving in this space, turn attention to the body and notice any physical sensations. Is there tension anywhere to be felt? If so, intentionally focus on it and relax it. You might even want to say to yourself, "relax," and then keep attention there. As the tension melts away, continue to shift awareness to other parts of the body and do the same.

Not only will you be driving in a much more peaceful state, you will also be practicing turning attention to the body instead of the mind dialog. To me, this is the simple art of mindful driving and provides great health benefits by relieving and preventing unnecessary stress. Indeed, by centering awareness on the body, you will head off any tension before it has the chance of causing physical damage later on, such as illness or injury. Importantly, it is unnoticed tension that causes stress on the body, compromising the immune system, along with leading to headaches, backaches and the like.

Next, let's consider what it means to eat mindfully. In the above paragraphs I have mentioned attending to the inner sensations of image, talk, and feeling, as well as the outer sense perception of touch, but I have yet to mention the other major sense perceptions relating to touch. Briefly, along with smell, taste belongs to the sense perception of touch, and like the physical sensations of the body, I have found it most helpful to practice it in action. In this case, it is the practice of mindful eating that helps us to get in touch (no pun intended) with the sense of taste and smell.

When you are sitting down to enjoy a meal, consider all that Mother Earth has provided to bring forth that which will nourish the body. Consider the soil full of minerals, and the water stored in clouds that is dispersed to the plant life that takes nutriment from the soil, combines it with energy from the sun, and converts it through photosynthesis so that it can be transferred to other organisms such as us. Then, consider all of the people who have coalesced to deliver the food to you, such as the farmer, the butcher, the trucker, the store clerk, etc.

After pausing to take in the wonder that brought the food to your plate, put all attention to the sense percepts that go along with it. First look at all the vibrant colors and textures. Take time to enjoy the aesthetic beauty of the sustenance you are about to consume. Next, put all attention to the smell. Try and notice all of the varying fragrances of the different provisions on the plate. Then, take a bite and let it sit in your mouth for a while. Feel the texture of the food against your tongue and the roof of your mouth.

As you begin to chew, notice all of the different flavors emanating from the bite of food. Continue to slowly chew and notice any changes in texture and flavor. After swallowing, clear your palate completely with the tongue, continuing to pay attention to the taste and feeling as you clean your mouth of the remnants of the bite. You might even consider rinsing your mouth with a little water after clearing the palate with the tongue. Then, repeat the above steps for each bite. Finally, give thanks to all those who consolidated to provide the meal for you, including Mother Earth.

I recommend practicing eating in this way at least once a week. Moreover, choose a meal that you really like, so that you can take the time to thoroughly enjoy it. You may find this practice to be quite delightful, as you will be afforded the opportunity to savor your favorite meal.

Finally, I would like to describe the practice of mindful walking. To me, mindful walking is an excellent practice for sharpening all the outer sensations of touch, sight and sound. For example, one day you can go on a 10-minute walk (or longer) and focus all attention on sight. When you look at a tree, or a bird, or a shrub, or anything else, just say to yourself "sight," and continue looking to the beauty of nature.

Similarly, on another day, you can focus all attention to that which you hear, and when you hear a bird, or a dog bark, or a car, or a plane overhead, just say "sound," and continue to listen. Or, you can turn all attention to your body, noticing what the ground feels like to your feet, and the air on your skin, and what your muscles feel like as you are walking. Then, every 8 to 10 seconds say to yourself, "touch," and continue to walk and notice any physical sensations you encounter, including the smell of fresh cut grass, or freshly bloomed flowers. You may be amazed at the peace you feel while attending to nature.

By practicing the art of mindful walking (along with mindful eating) and tuning into the Mother Earth, not only will you gain a sense of the peace that is innate to all of nature, you will also gain an appreciation and greater reverence for life. In turn, you will be helping the entire planet. I fully believe it all begins with gaining a greater appreciation for what our Mother Earth has provided in support of all our lives. Moreover, that begins with mindful awareness in all we do. So remain present, and be here now!

BIBLIOGRAPHY

Csikszentmihalyi, Mihaly. *Flow: The Psychology of Optimal Experience.* New York, NY: HarperCollins Publishing, 1990. Print.

Chopra, Deepak. *Ageless Body, Timeless Mind.* New York, NY: Three Rivers Press. 1998. Print.

Dyer, Wayne W. *Manifest Your Destiny.* New York, NY: HarperCollins Publishing, 1997. Print.

Dyer, Wayne W. *Your Sacred Self.* New York, NY: HarperCollins Publishing, 1995. Print.

Dyer, Wayne W. *Your Erroneous Zones.* New York, NY: HarperCollins Publishing. 1976. Print.

Feuerstein, Georg. *The Bhagavad-Gita, A New Translation.* Boston, MA: Shambhala Publishing Inc. 2011. Print.

Goleman, D., Lipton, B. H., Pert, C., Small, G., Braden, G., and Achterberg, J. *Measuring the Immeasurable: The Scientific Case for Spirituality.* Boulder, CO: Sounds True Incorporated. 2008. Print.

Goleman, Daniel. *Destructive Emotions: How Can We Overcome Them?* New York, NY: Bantam Publishing. 2003. Print.

Jung, C. G. *Psychology and Religion: West and East.* (Trans Gerhard Adler & R. F. C. Hull). Princeton, NJ: Princeton University Press, 2nd edition. 1969. Print.

Jung, C. G. *The Undiscovered Self.* (Trans R. F. C. Hull, 1990). Princeton, NJ: Princeton University Press, 1957. Print.

Jung, C. G. *Modern Man in Search of a Soul*. Orlando, FL: Harcourt Inc., 1933. Print.

Kriyananda, Swami. *The Essence of the Bhagavad-Gita*. Nevada City, CA: Crystal Clarity Publishers. 2006. Print.

Megre, Vladimir. *The Book of Kin*. (Trans John Woodsworth). Kahului, HI: Ringing Cedars Press, 2008. Print.

Mitchell, Stephen. *The Second Book of the Tao*. New York, NY: The Penguin Press. 2009. Print.

MSI. *Enlightenment: The Yoga Sutras of Patanjali, a New Translation and Commentary*. Waynesville, NC: SFA Publications. 1995. Print.

Peck, Scott M. *Further Along the Road Less Traveled*. New York, NY: Simon & Schuster. 1993. Print.

Tolle, Eckhart. *A New Earth: Awakening to Your Life's Purpose*. New York, NY: Plume Publishing. 2005. Print.

Tolle, Eckhart. *The Power of Now*. Vancouver, Canada: Namaste Publishing. 1999. Print.

Wolinsky, Stephen. *Quantum Consciousness: The Guide To Experiencing Quantum Psychology*. North Bergen, NJ: Bramble Books Publishing, 1993. Print.

Yogananda, Paramahansa. *The Yoga of Jesus*. Los Angeles, CA: Self-Realization Fellowship. 2004. Print.

Zukav, Gary, & Francis, Linda. *The Mind of the Soul*. New York, NW: Free Press Publishing, 2003.

About the Author

Jeffry C. Beers is an author and former teacher and coach. He holds a Master's Degree in Education from the University of Portland and a Master's Degree in Psychology from Portland State University, where he also received training in Mindfulness. Jeffry has written seven books addressing the topic of 'present moment awareness' and is currently working on an eighth. His experience in education, along with the last ten years of studying the ancient teachings in philosophy, theology, and spirituality, have led him to a desire to pass along his knowledge and story with others.